Thanks to Jimmy Beaulieu, Jeffrey Brown, Julie Dubé, and Lewis Trondheim
— PASCAL GIRARD

Drawn & Quarterly
Post Office Box 48056
Montreal, Quebec
Canada H2V 4S8
www.drawnandquarterly.com

First edition: December 2008.
Printed in Canada.

10 9 8 7 6 5 4 3 2 1

Library and Archives Canada Cataloguing in Publication
Girard, Pascal
    Nicolas / Pascal Girard ; translator: Helge Dascher.
Translation of Nicolas. Originally published in French by Mécanique Générale
(Montreal, 2006).
ISBN 978-1-897299-71-5
    I. Dascher, Helge, 1965- II. Title.
PN6733.G57N5313 2008   741.5'971   C2008-907206-5

Drawn & Quarterly acknowledges the financial contribution of the Government
of Canada through the Book Publishing Industry Development Program (BPIDP)
and the Canada Council for the Arts for our publishing activities and for support
of this edition.

Distributed in the USA by:
Farrar, Straus and Giroux, 18 West 18th Street, New York, NY 10011
Orders: 888.330.8477

Distributed in Canada by:
Raincoast Books, 9050 Shaughnessy Street, Vancouver, BC V6P 6E5
Orders: 800.663.5714

Printed by Imprimerie Transcontinental in Sherbrooke, Quebec, November 2008.

Translated by Helge Dascher

nicolas

DRAWN AND QUARTERLY

petits livres

BEFORE

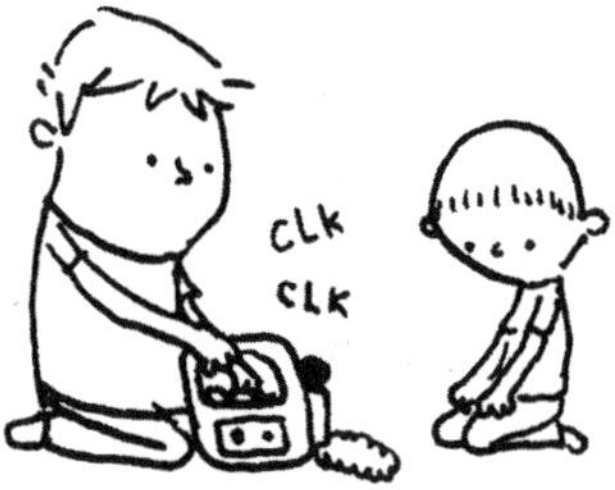
CLK
CLK

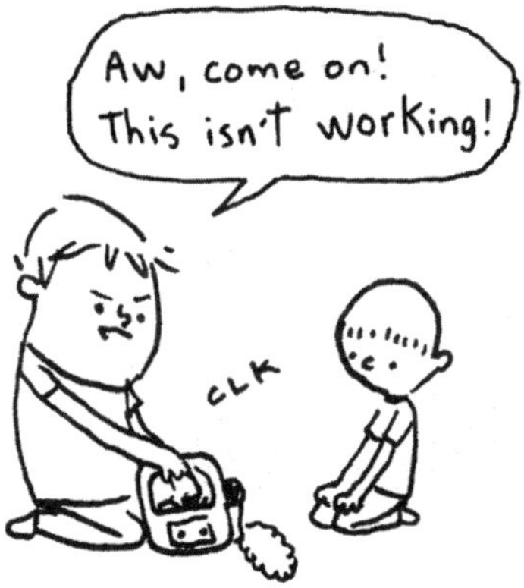
Aw, come on! This isn't working!
CLK

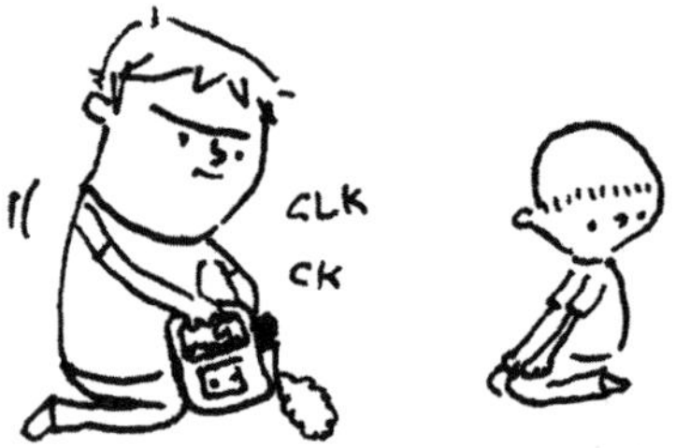
CLK
CK

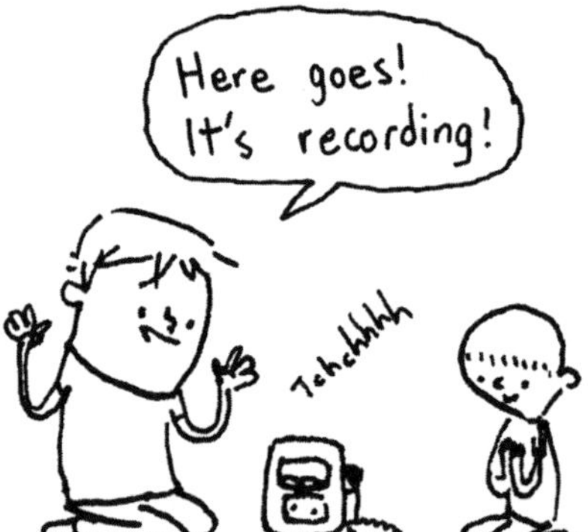
Here goes! It's recording!
Tchchhhh

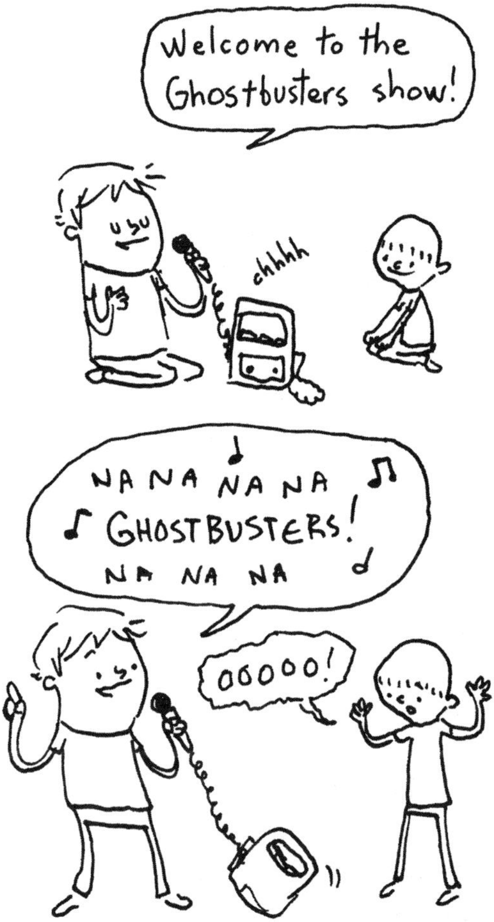
Welcome to the Ghostbusters show!
chhhh
NA NA NA NA GHOSTBUSTERS! NA NA NA
OOOOO!

AFTER

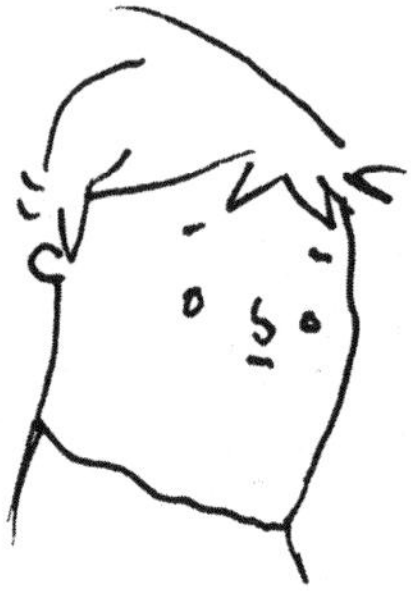

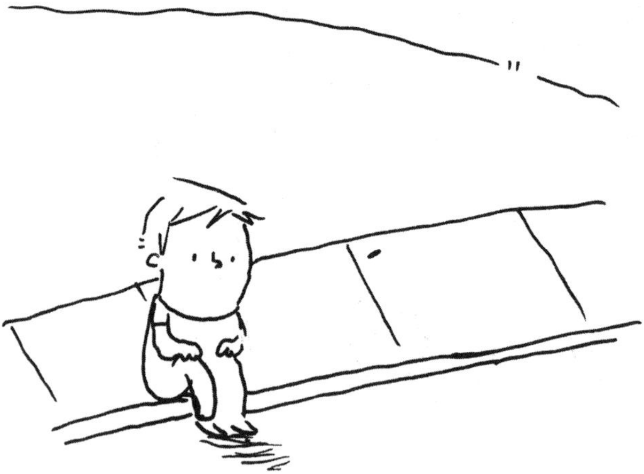

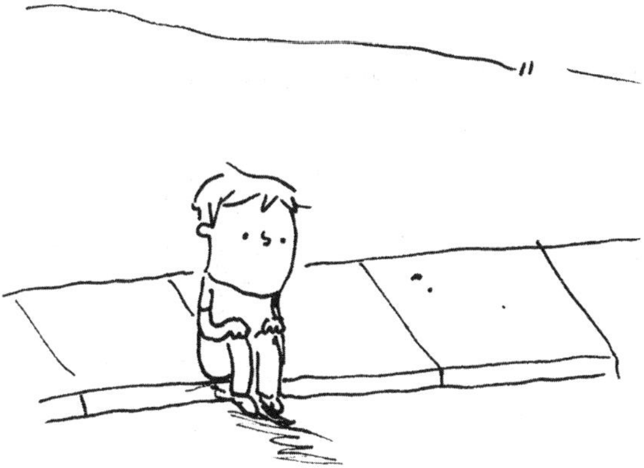

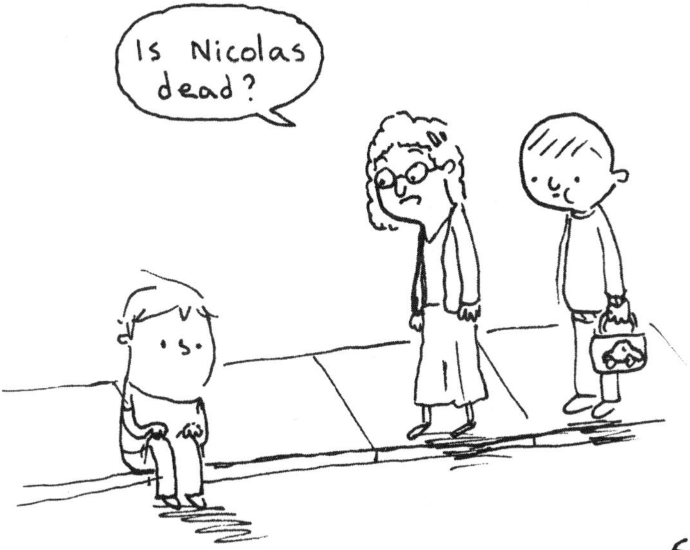
Is Nicolas dead?

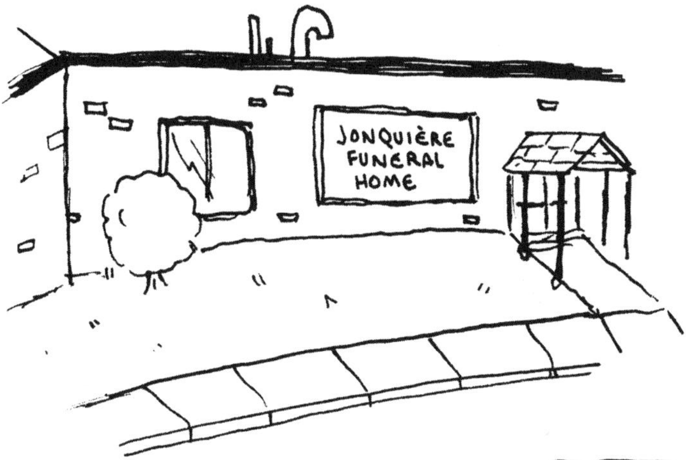
JONQUIÈRE
FUNERAL
HOME

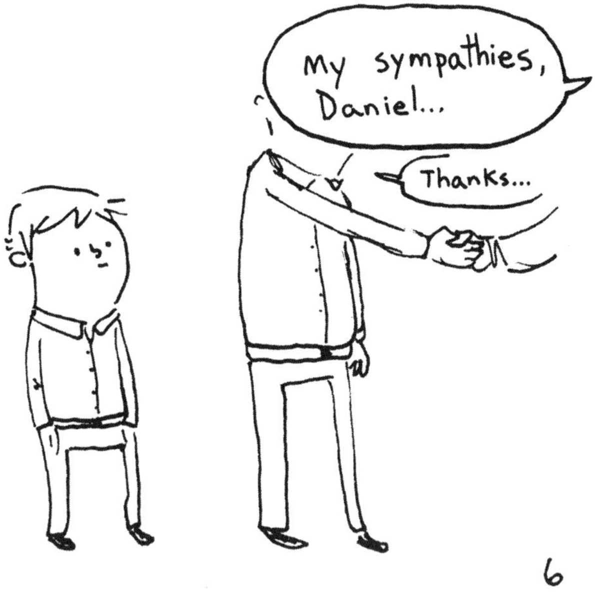
My sympathies, Daniel...
Thanks...

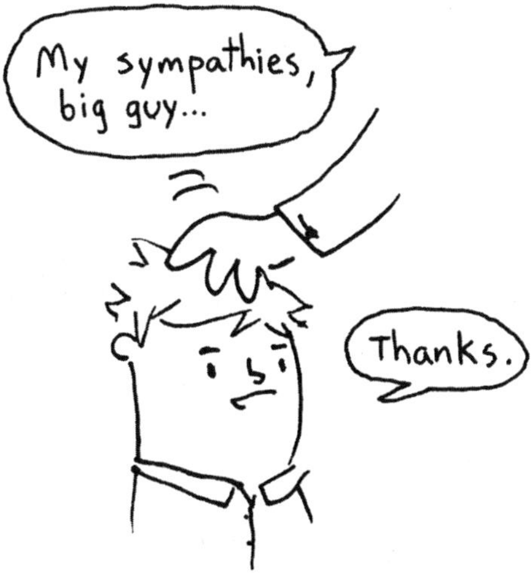
My sympathies, big guy...
Thanks.

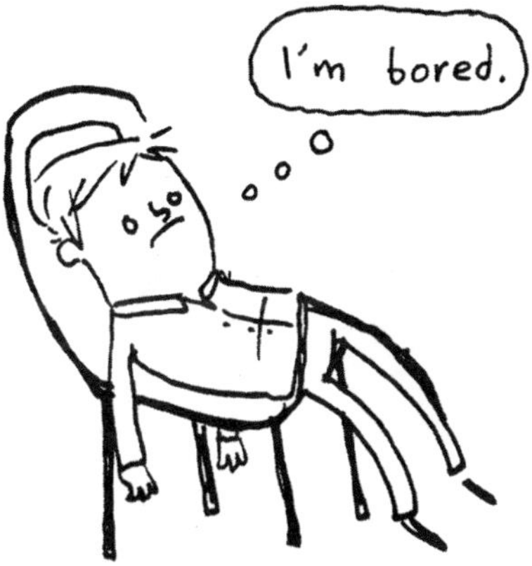
I'm bored.

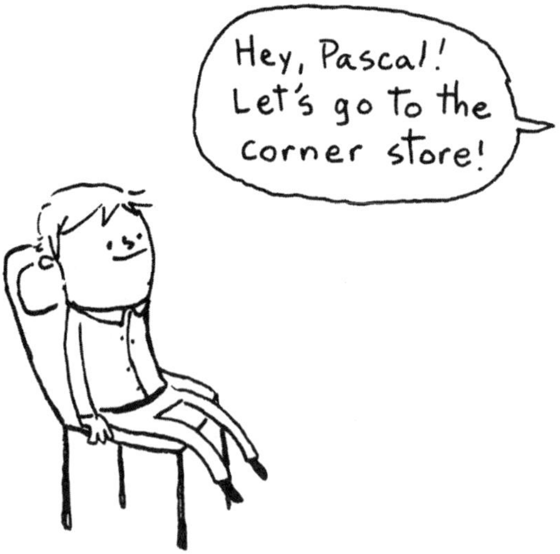
Hey, Pascal! Let's go to the corner store!

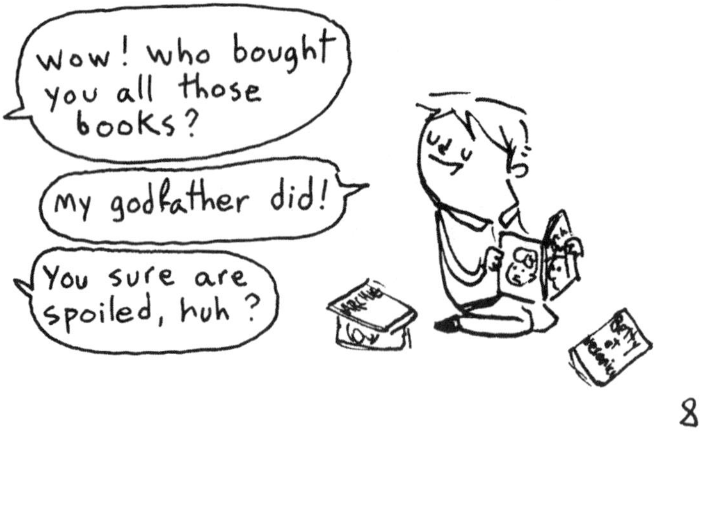
wow! who bought you all those books?
My godfather did!
You sure are spoiled, huh?

Your new video game is cool!
How come your brother's dead?
I dunno.

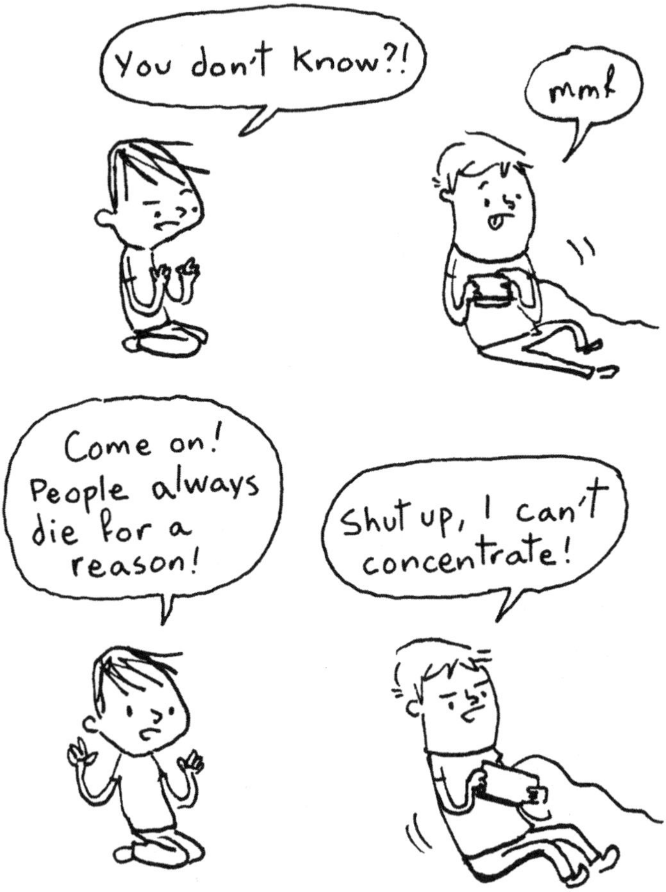
You don't know?!
mmf
Come on! People always die for a reason!
Shut up, I can't concentrate!

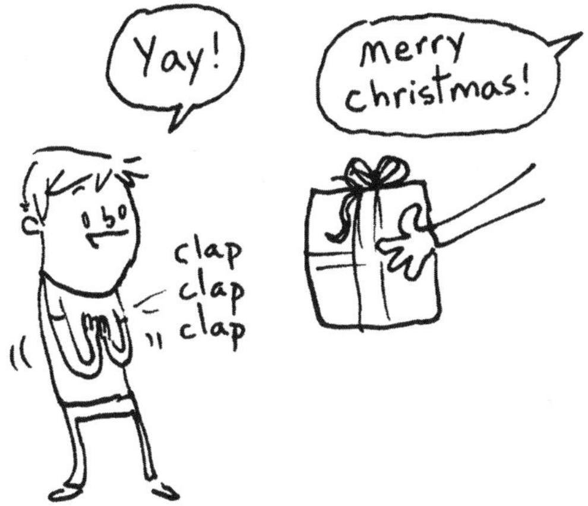
Yay!
merry christmas!
clap
clap
clap

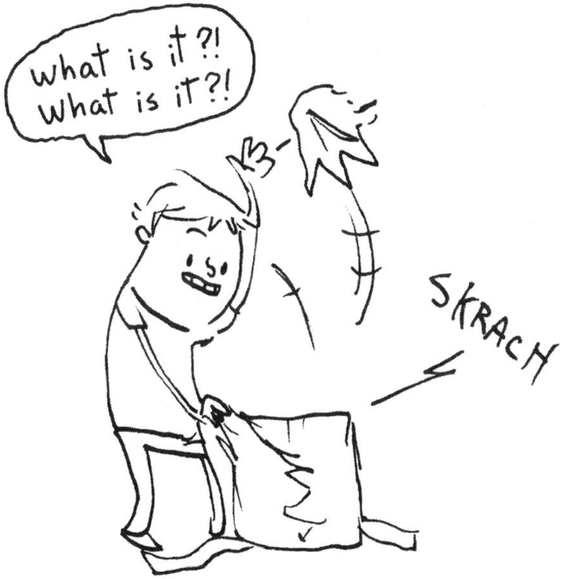
what is it?!
what is it?!
SKRACH

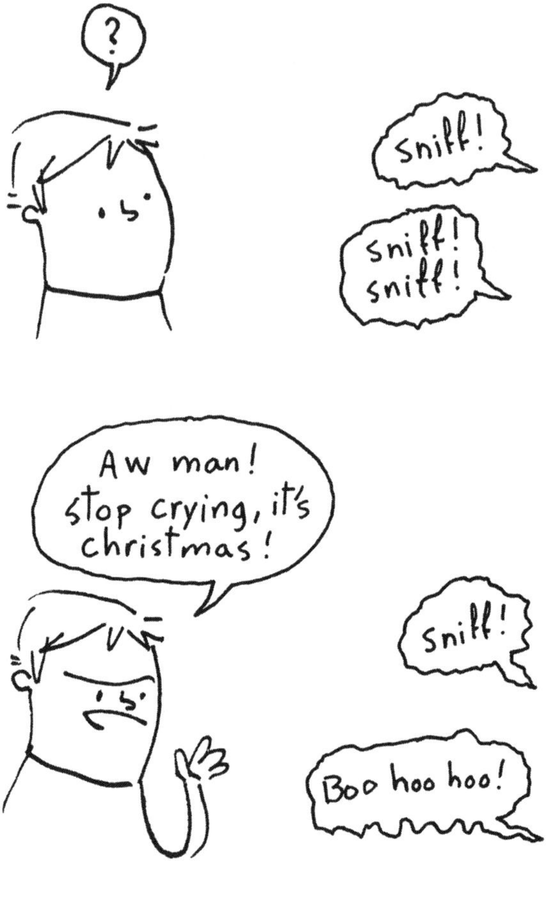
?
Sniff!
Sniff! sniff!
Aw man! stop crying, it's christmas!
Sniff!
Boo hoo hoo!

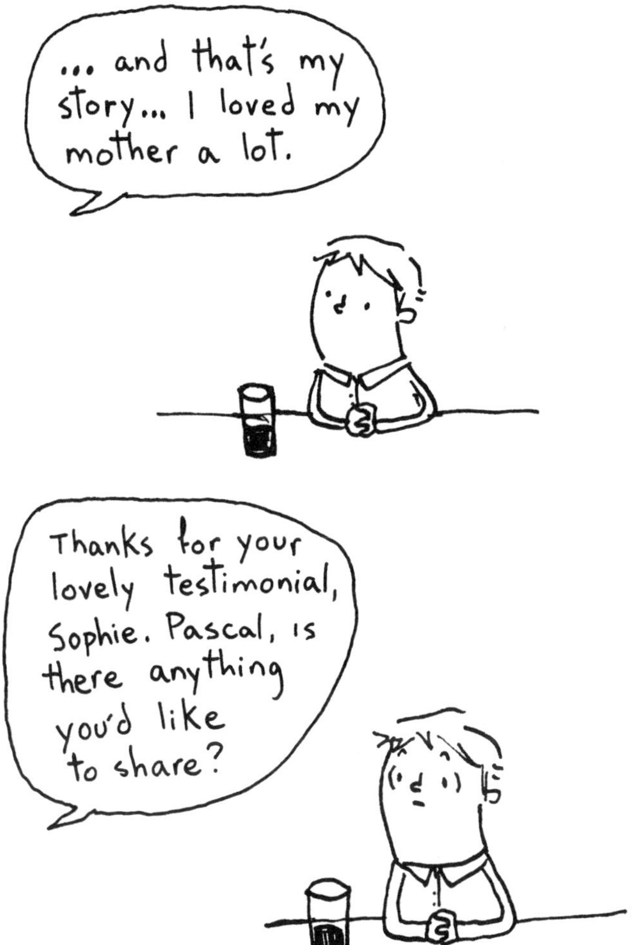
... and that's my story... I loved my mother a lot.
Thanks for your lovely testimonial, Sophie. Pascal, is there anything you'd like to share?

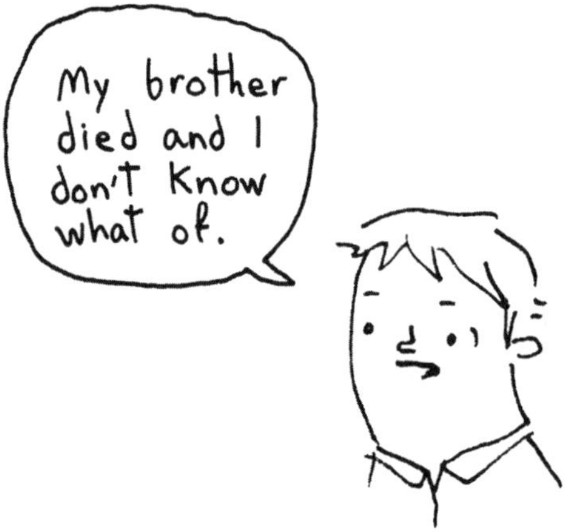
My brother died and I don't know what of.

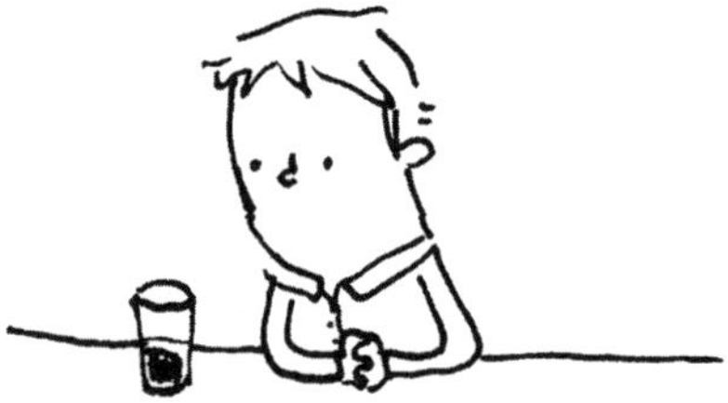

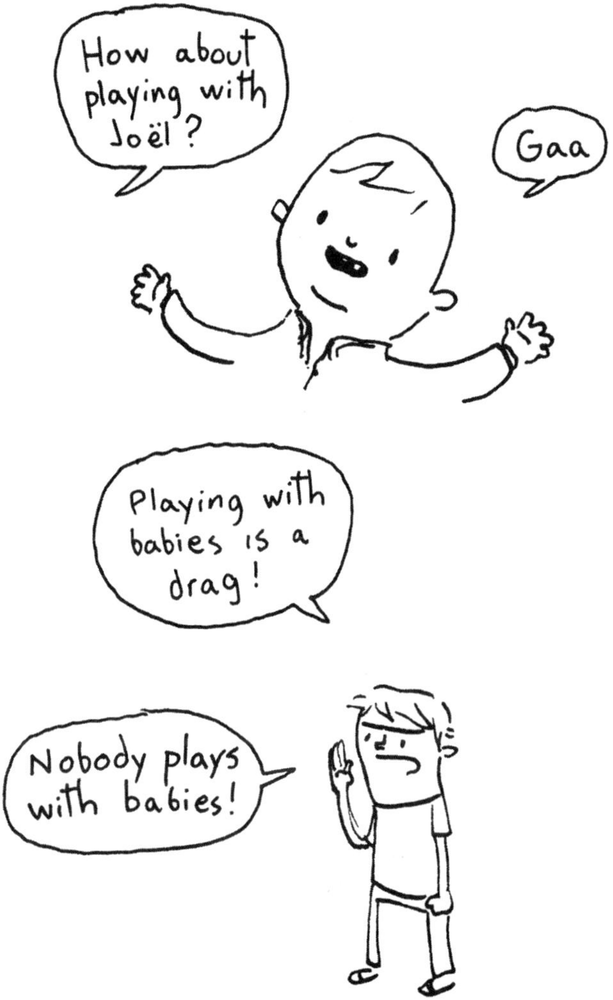
How about playing with Joël?
Gaa
Playing with babies is a drag!
Nobody plays with babies!

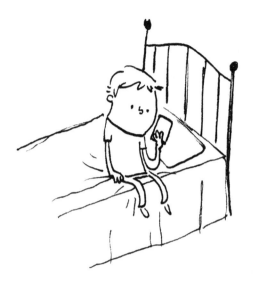

16

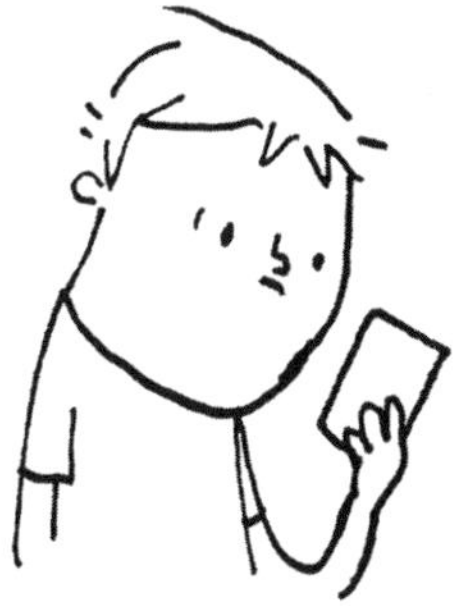

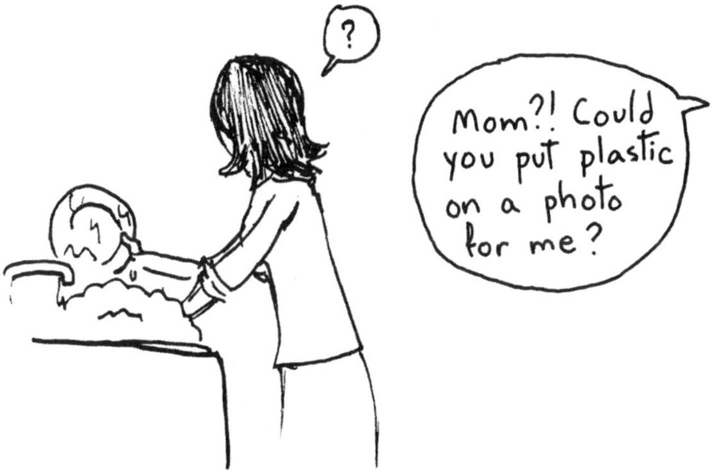
?
Mom?! Could you put plastic on a photo for me?

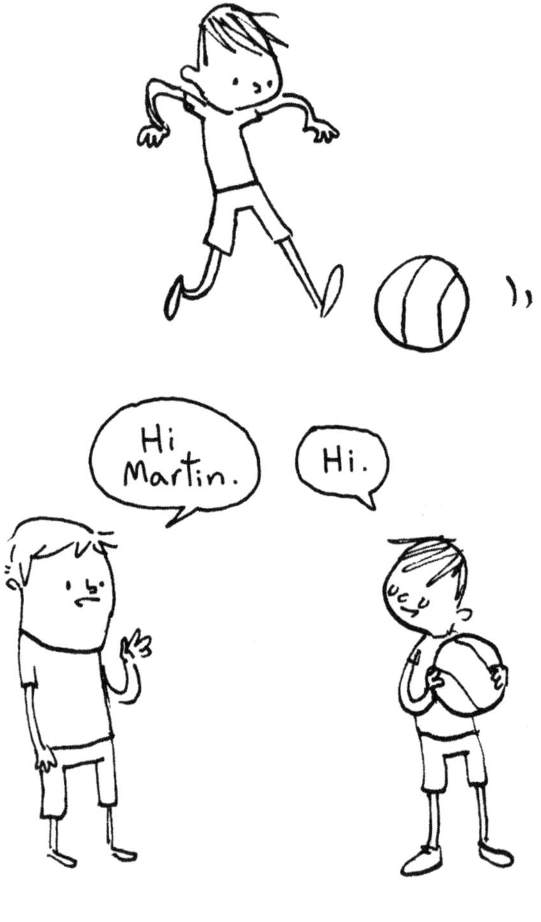
Hi Martin.
Hi.

The doctor said my brother died of lactic acidosis.
What's that?

20

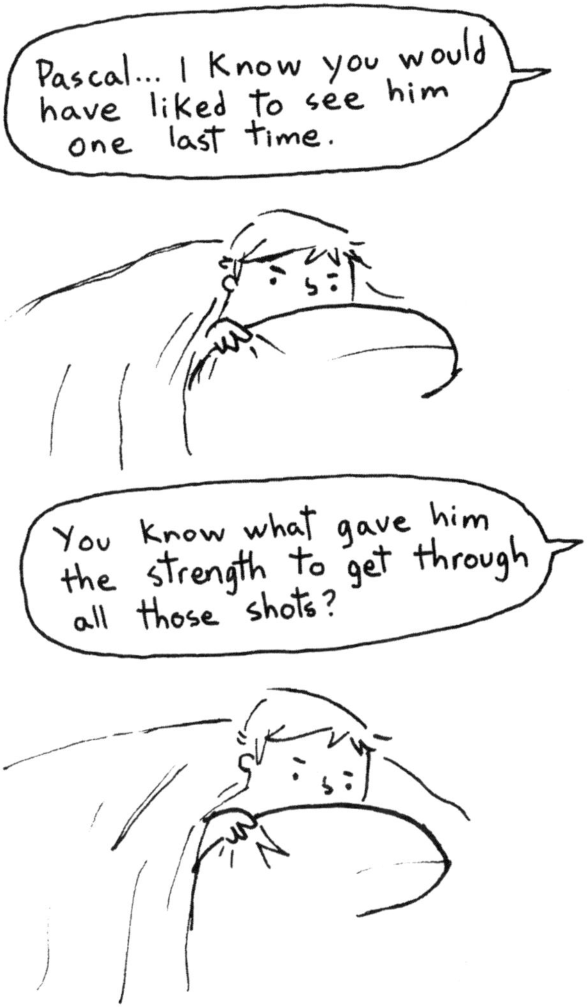
Pascal... I know you would have liked to see him one last time.
You know what gave him the strength to get through all those shots?

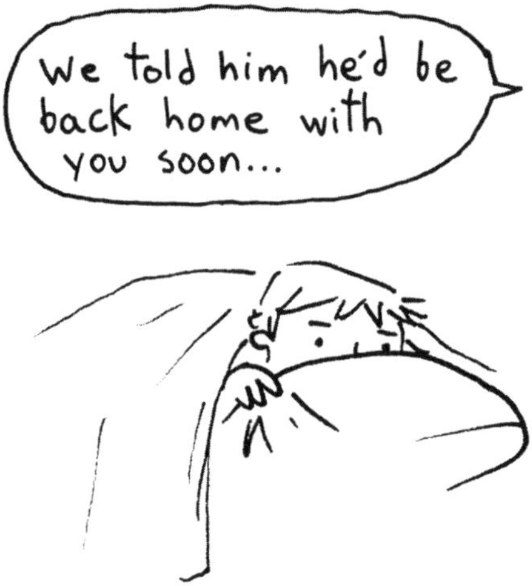
We told him he'd be back home with you soon...

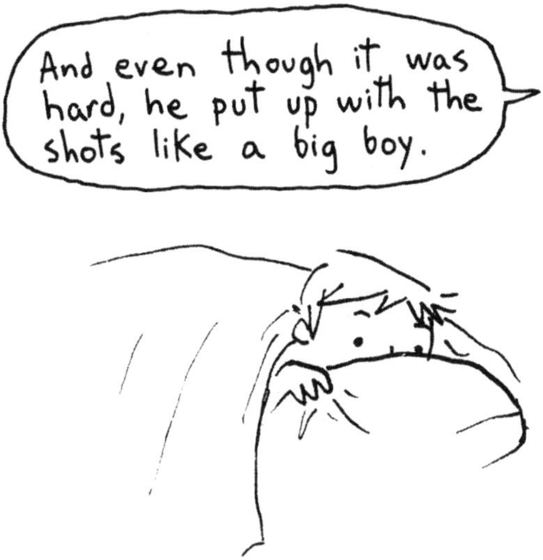
And even though it was hard, he put up with the shots like a big boy.

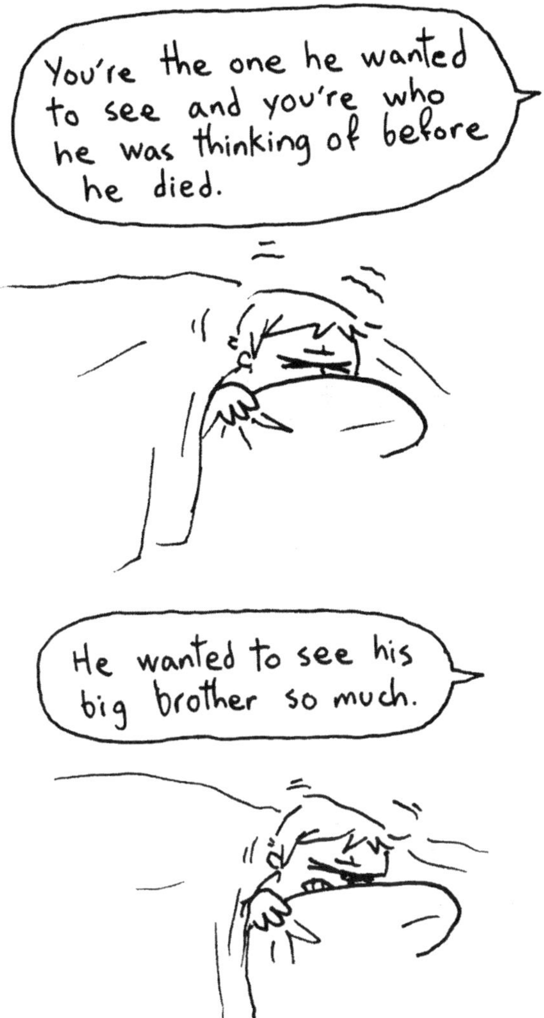
You're the one he wanted to see and you're who he was thinking of before he died.
He wanted to see his big brother so much.

If we'd known...

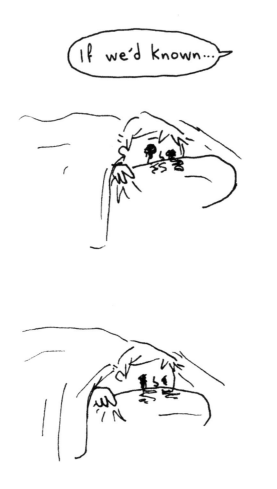

Tchiik
Tchiik

25

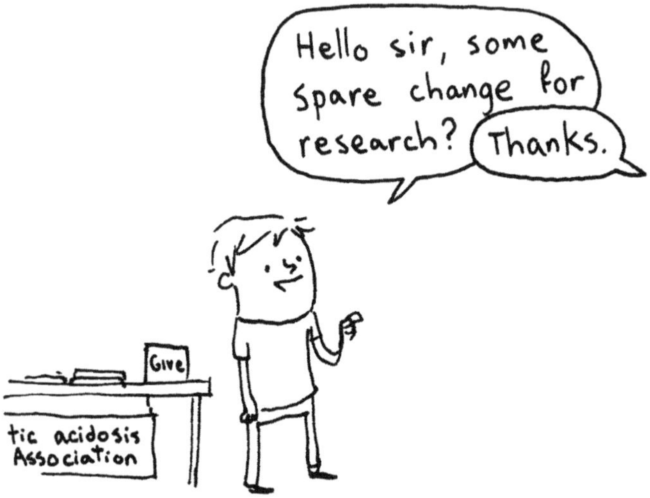
Hello sir, some spare change for research?
Thanks.
Give
tic acidosis Association

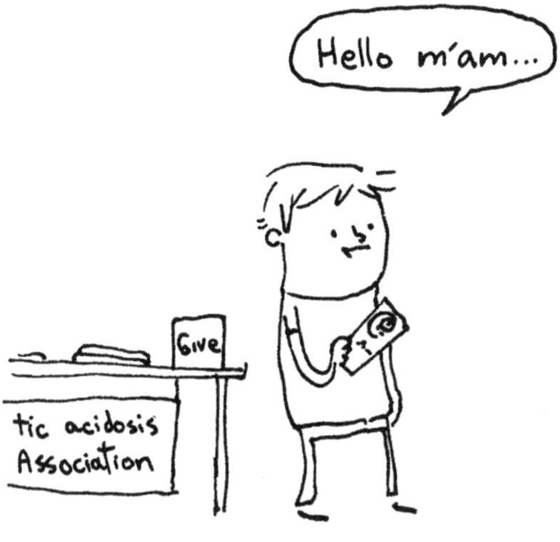
Hello m'am...
Give
tic acidosis Association

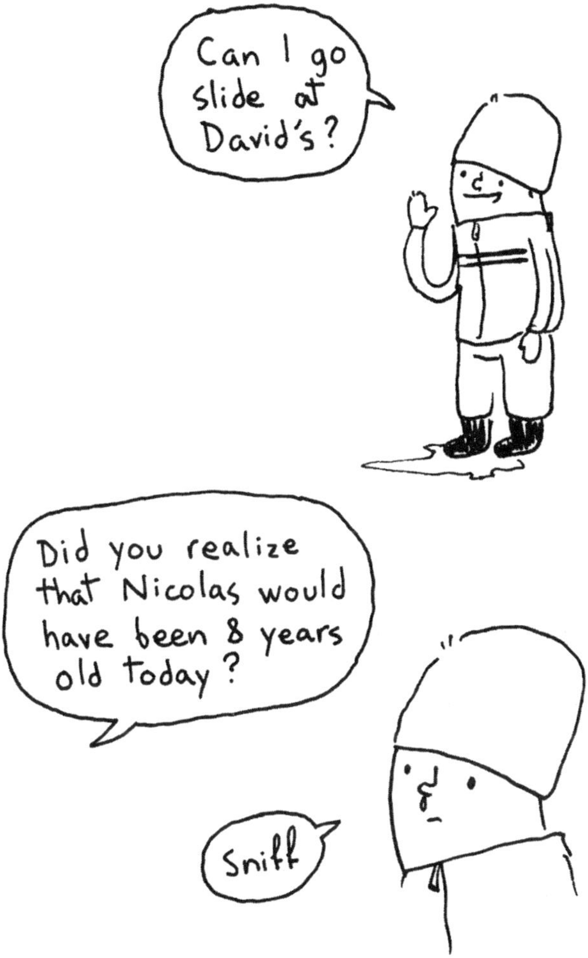
Can I go slide at David's?
Did you realize that Nicolas would have been 8 years old today?
Sniff

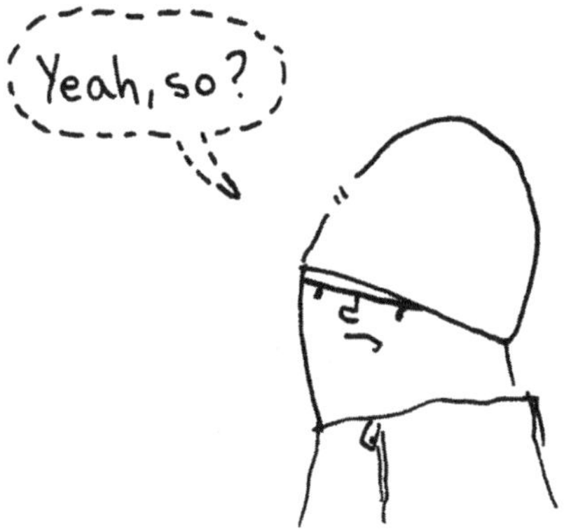
Yeah, so?

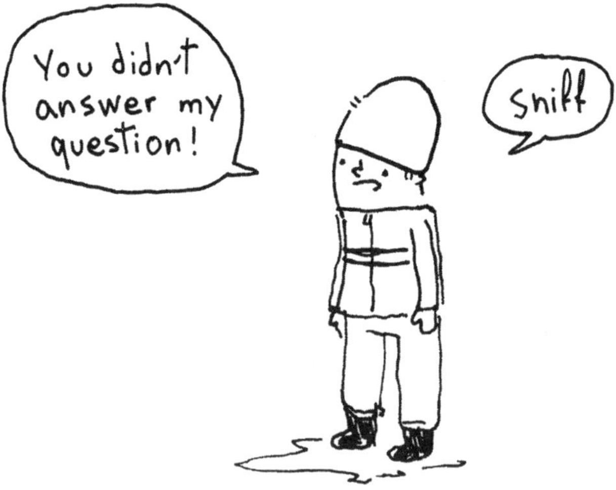
You didn't answer my question!
Sniff

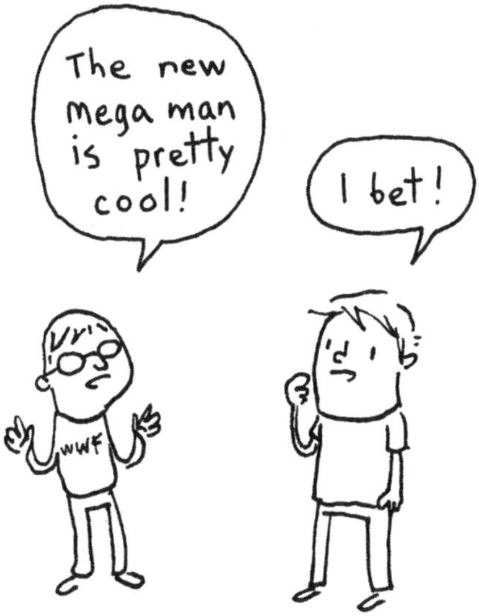
The new mega man is pretty cool!
I bet!
WWF

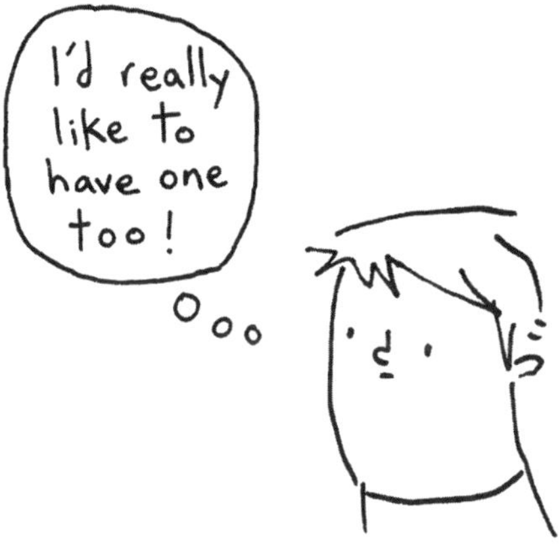
I'd really like to have one too!

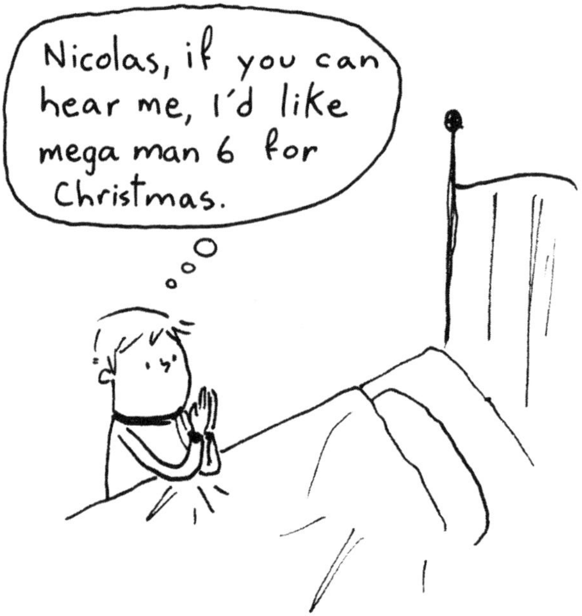
Nicolas, if you can hear me, I'd like mega man 6 for Christmas.

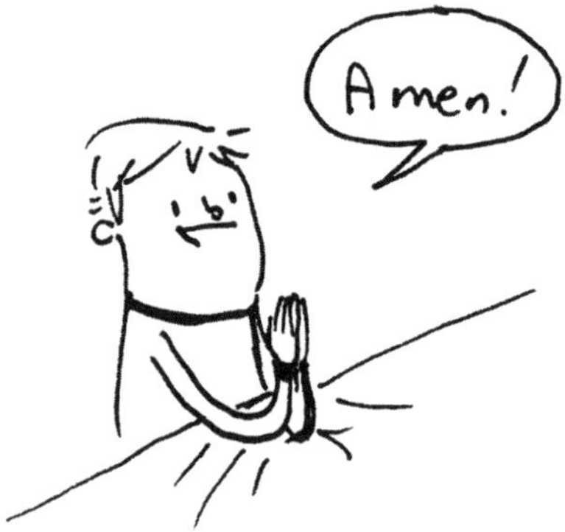
Amen!

Tomorrow,
high
School.

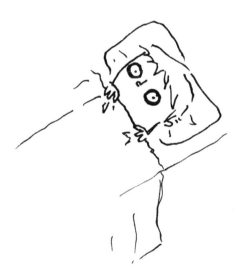

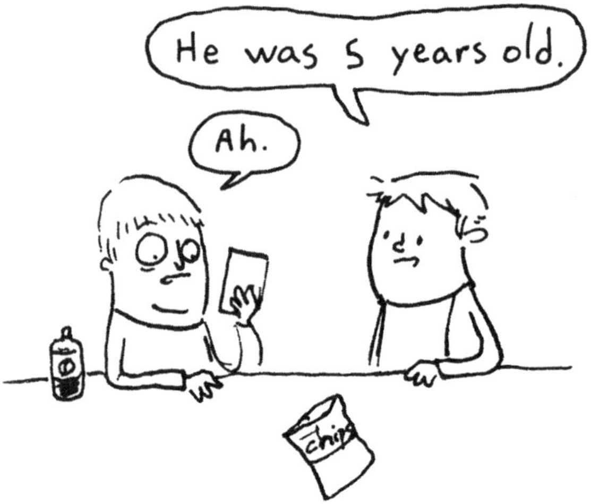
Ah.
He was 5 years old.
chips

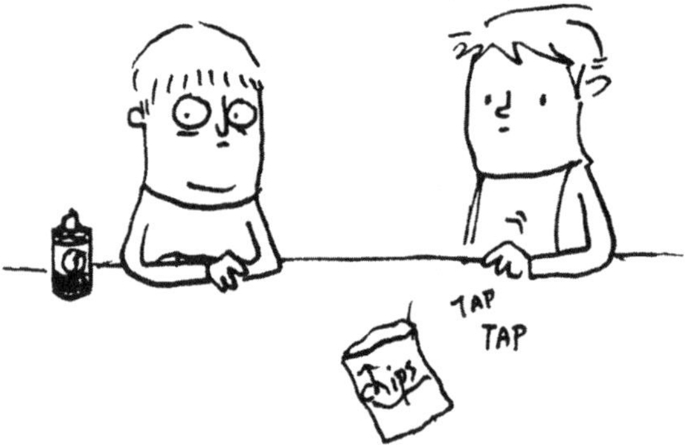
TAP
TAP
chips

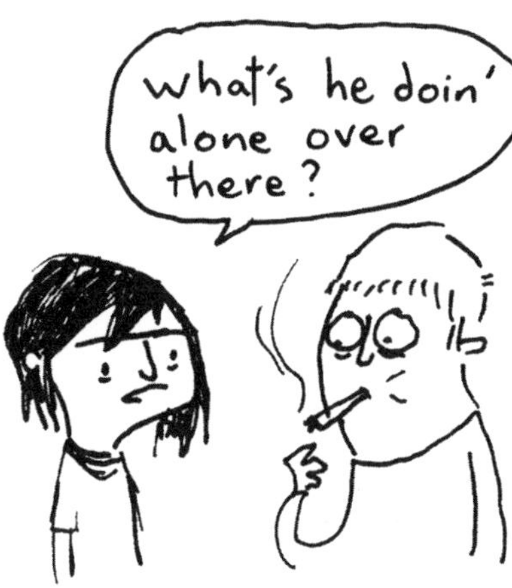
what's he doin' alone over there?

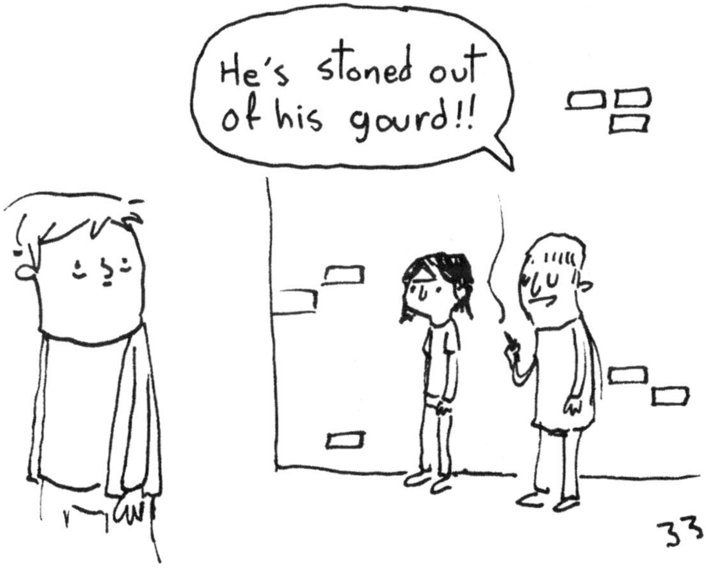
He's stoned out of his gourd!!

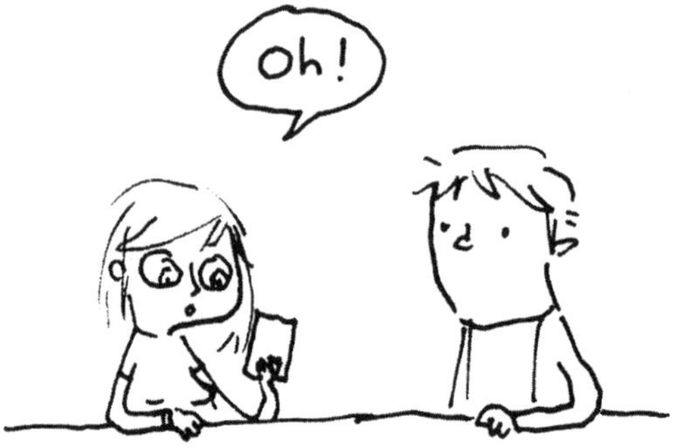
Oh!

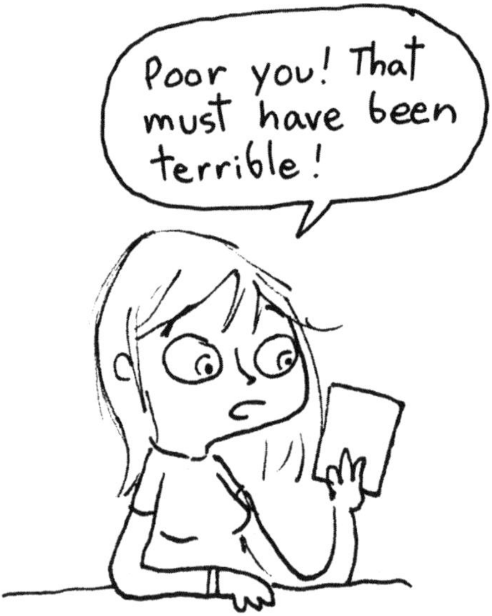
Poor you! That must have been terrible!

For sure...but...
that's life, I guess...

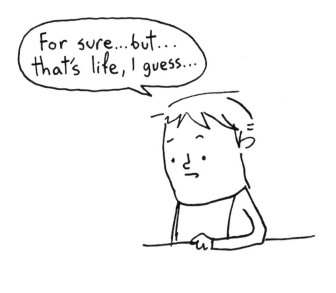

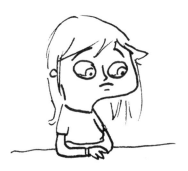

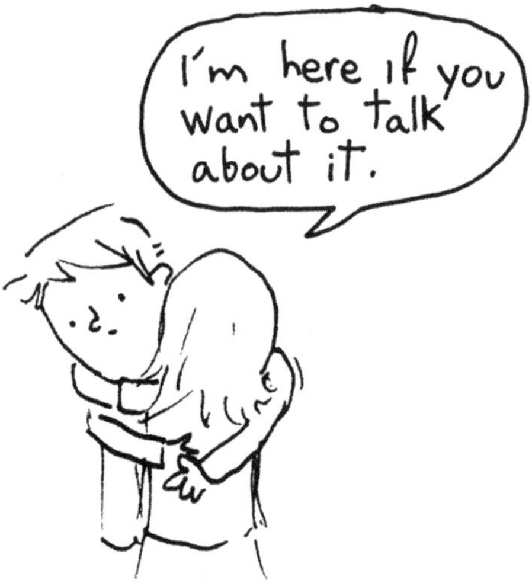
I'm here if you want to talk about it.

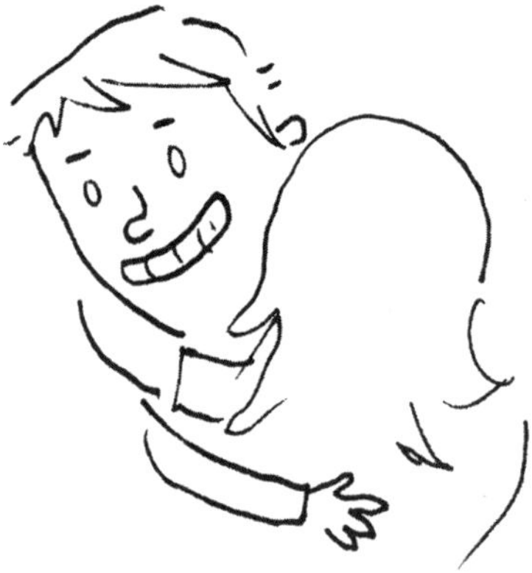

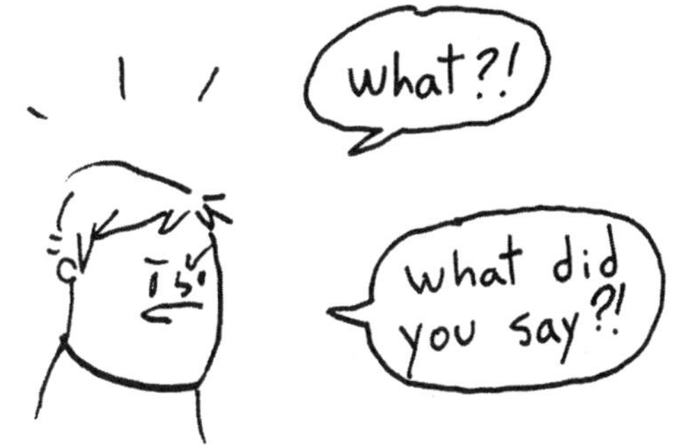
what?!
what did you say?!

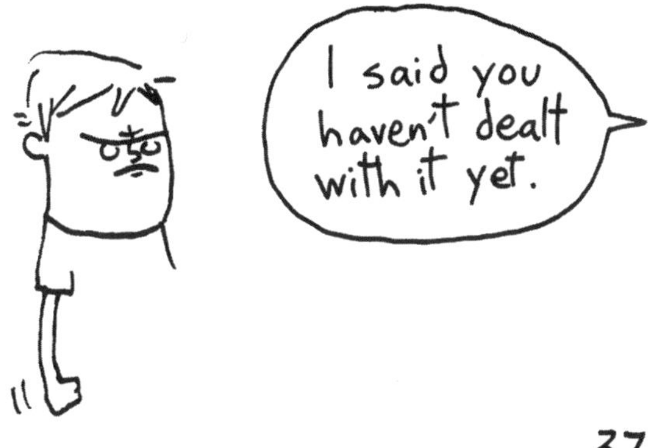
I said you haven't dealt with it yet.

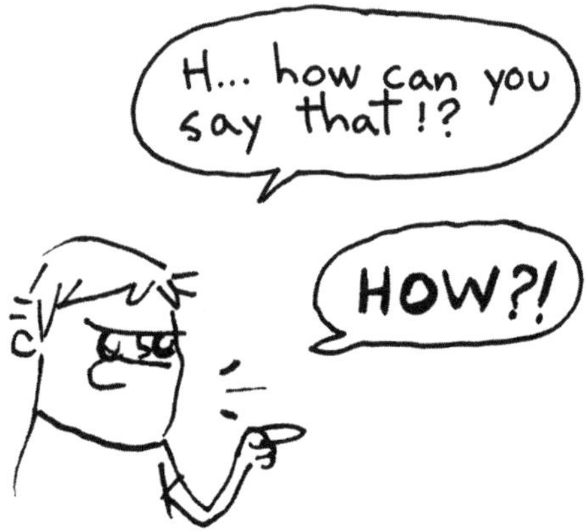
H... how can you say that!?
HOW?!

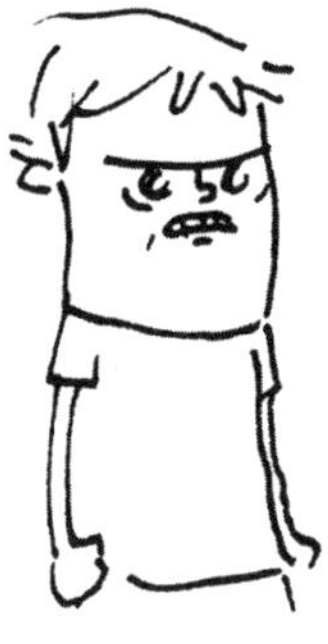

39

40

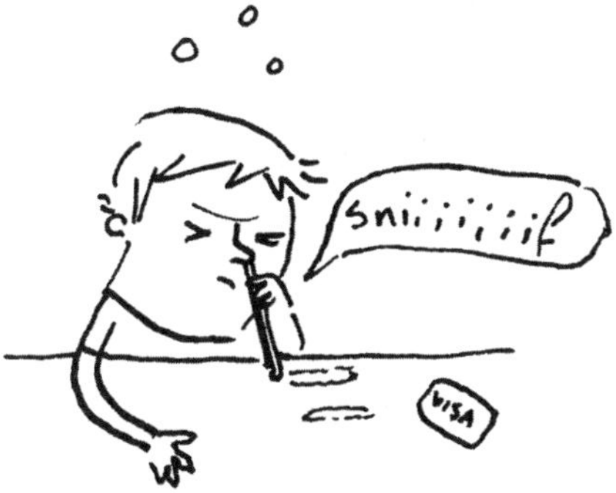
Sniiiiiiiif
VISA

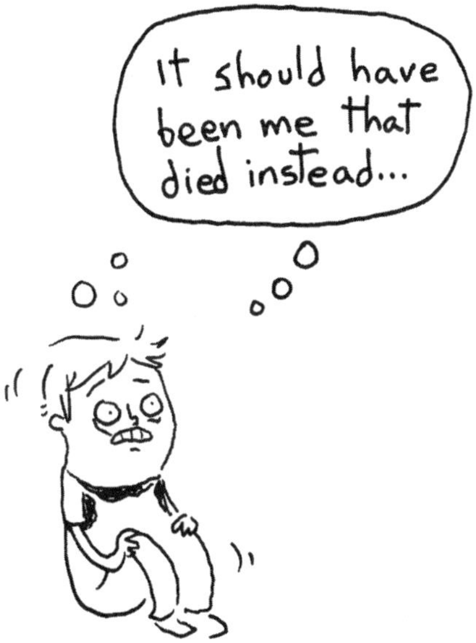
It should have been me that died instead...

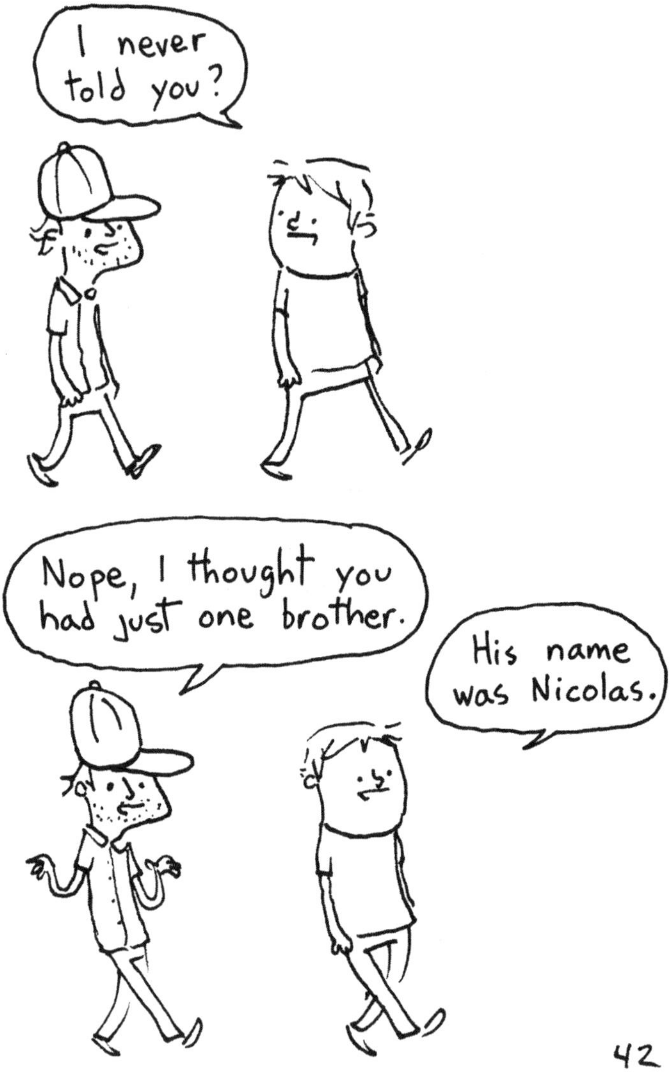
I never told you?
Nope, I thought you had just one brother.
His name was Nicolas.

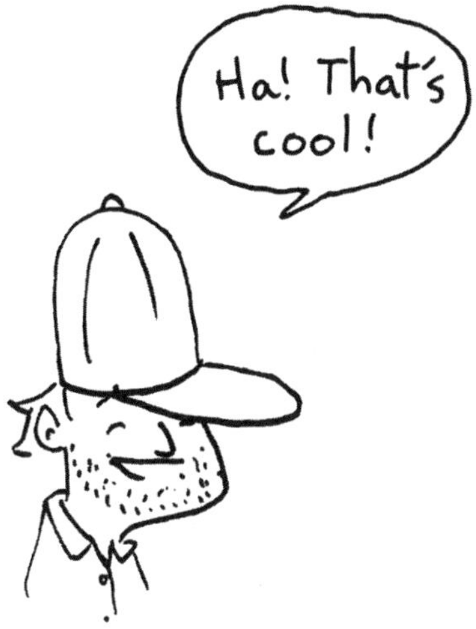
Ha! That's cool!

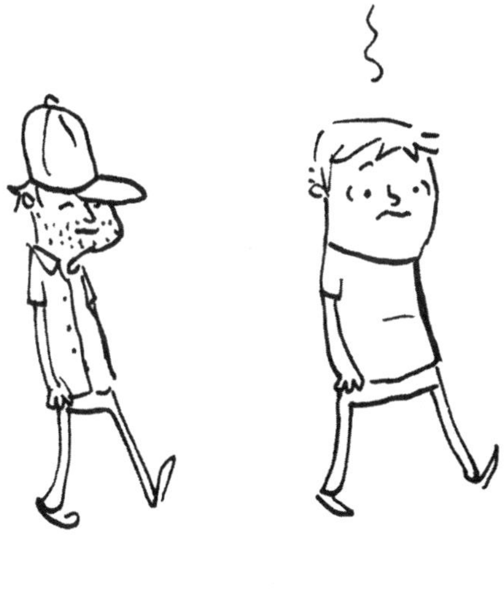

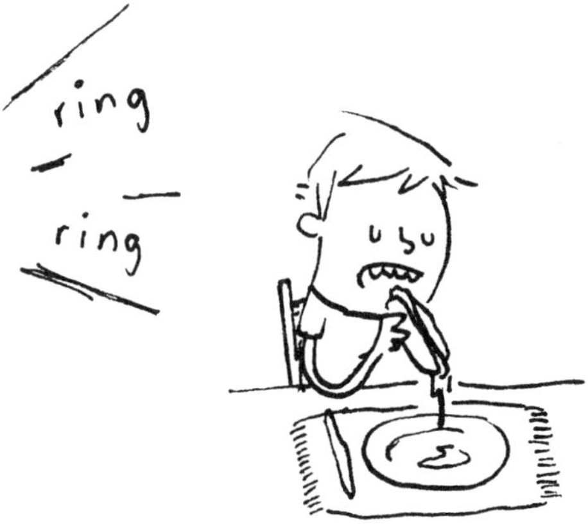
ring
ring

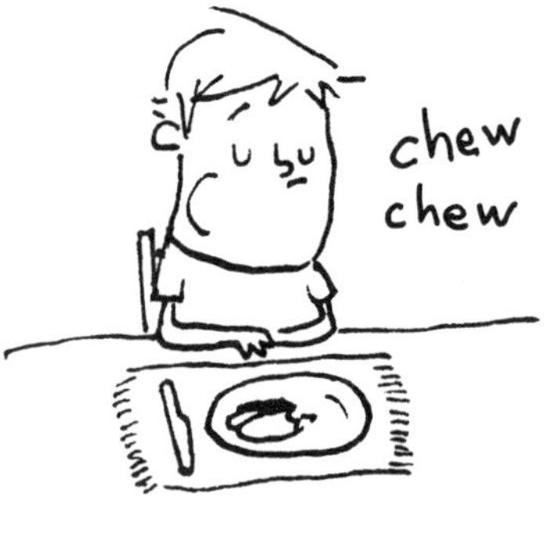
chew
chew

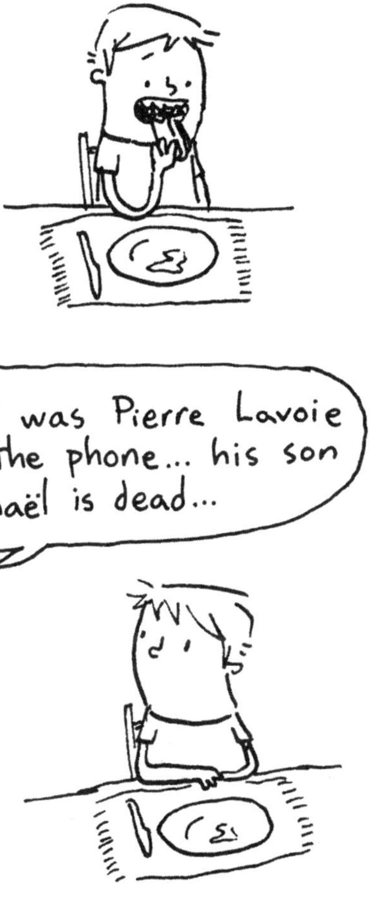
That was Pierre Lavoie on the phone... his son Raphaël is dead...

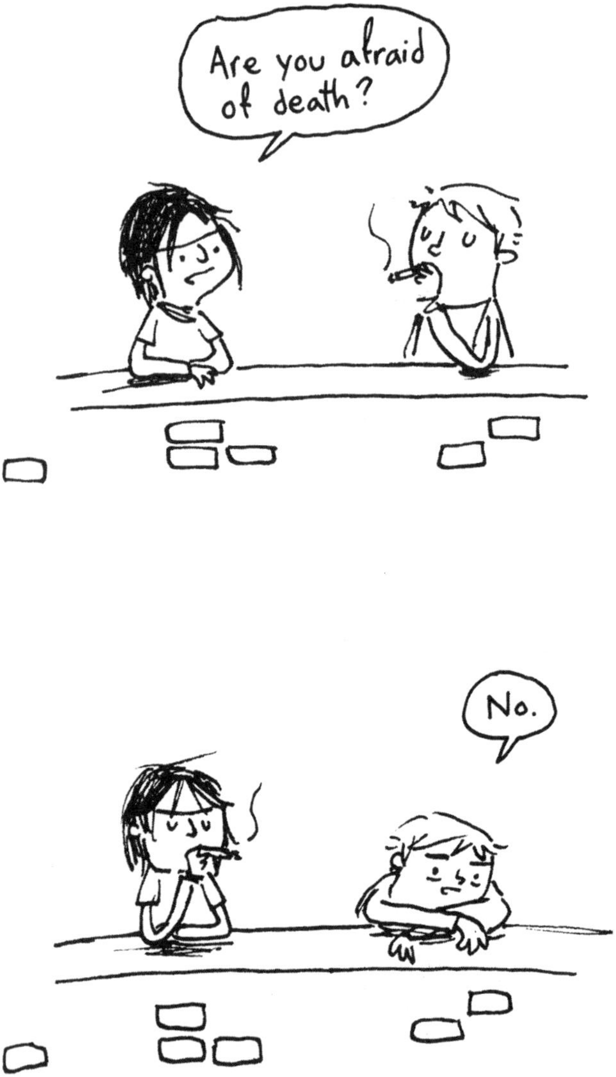
Are you afraid of death?
No.

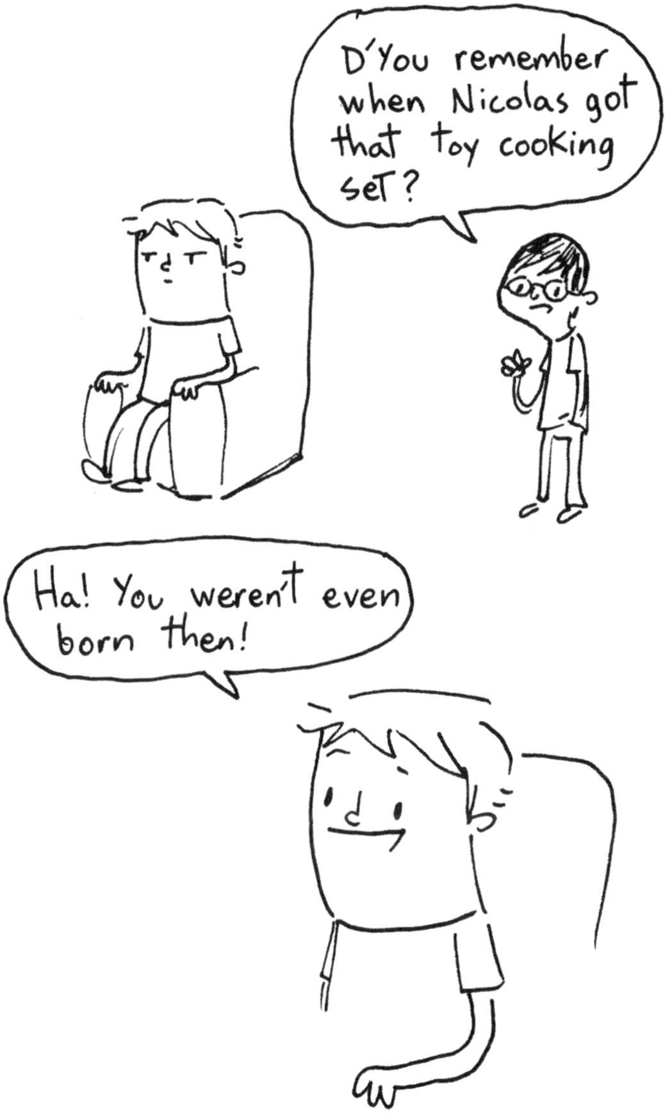
D'You remember when Nicolas got that toy cooking set?
Ha! You weren't even born then!

Yes I was! He said: "I'm gonna go cook something!"

You saw that in a video!!

49

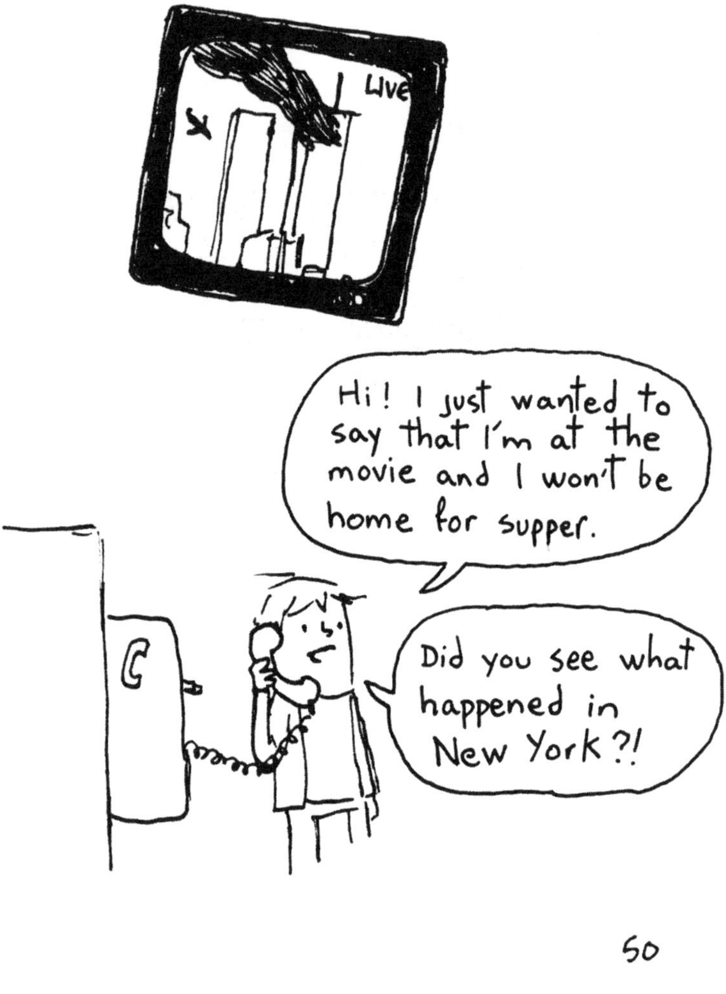
LIVE
Hi! I just wanted to say that I'm at the movie and I won't be home for supper.
Did you see what happened in New York?!

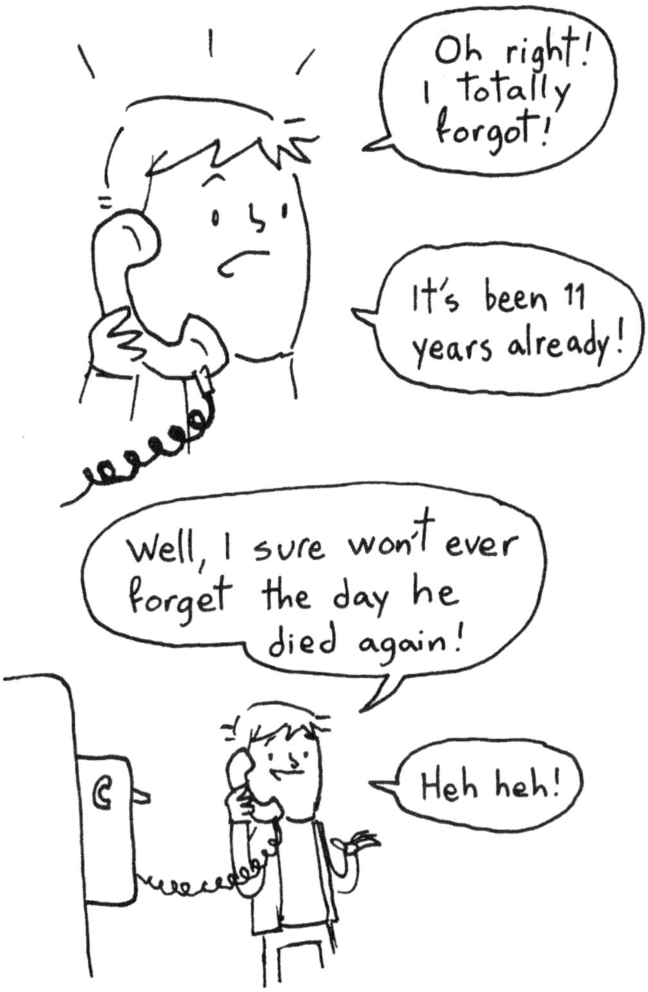
Oh right! I totally forgot!
It's been 11 years already!
Well, I sure won't ever forget the day he died again!
Heh heh!

I can't even remember what his voice sounded like.

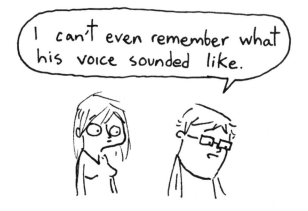

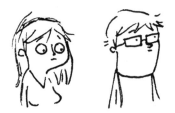

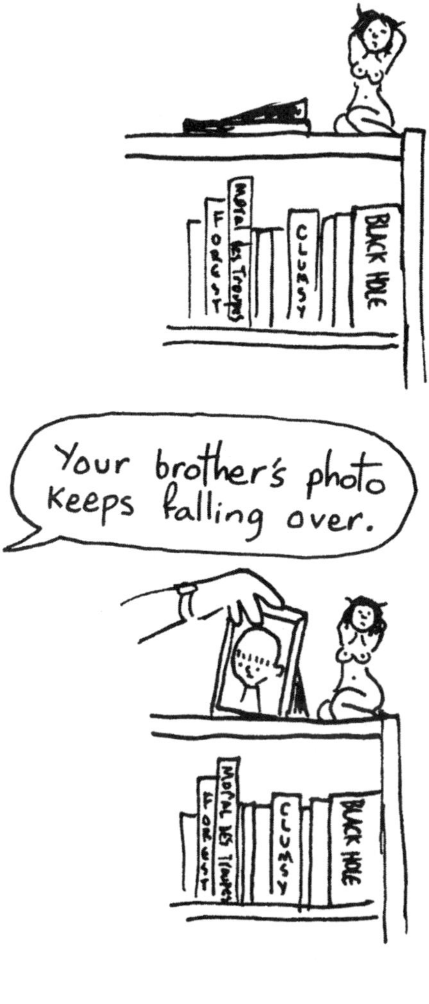
FOREST
CLUMSY
BLACK HOLE
Your brother's photo keeps falling over.

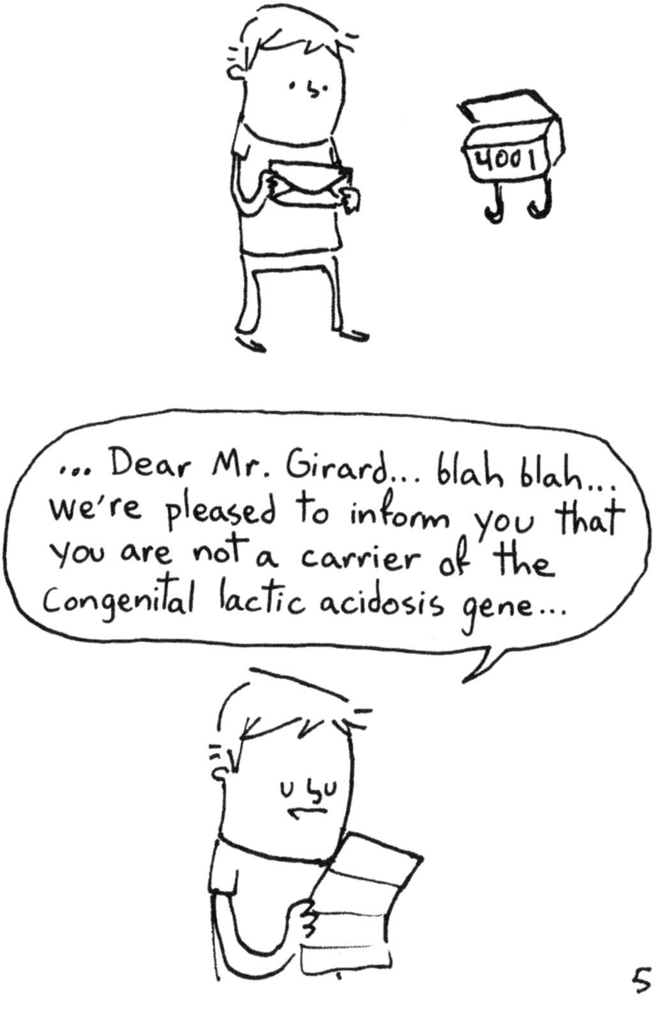
4001
... Dear Mr. Girard... blah blah... we're pleased to inform you that you are not a carrier of the Congenital lactic acidosis gene...

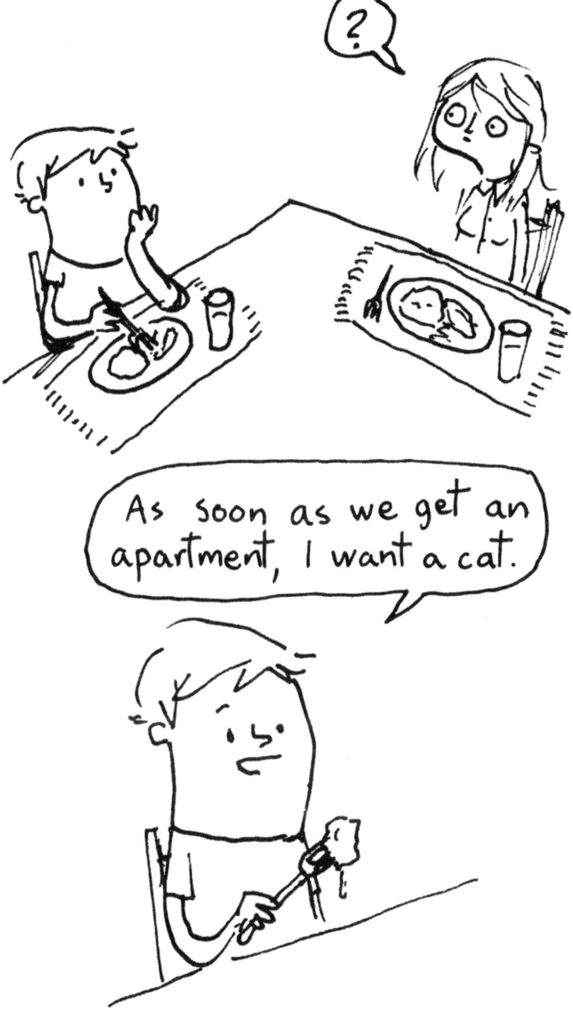
?
As soon as we get an apartment, I want a cat.

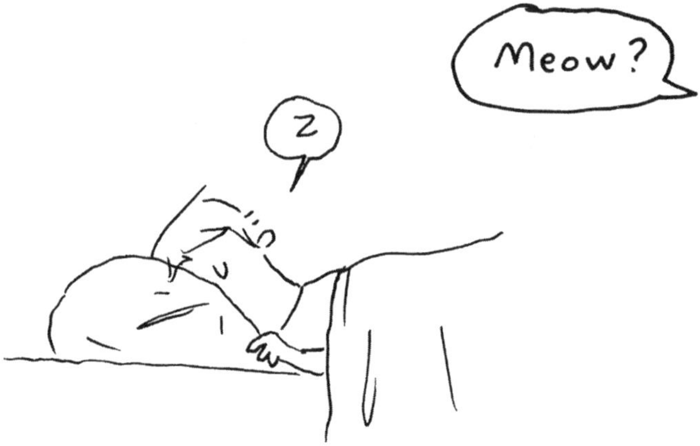
Meow?
z

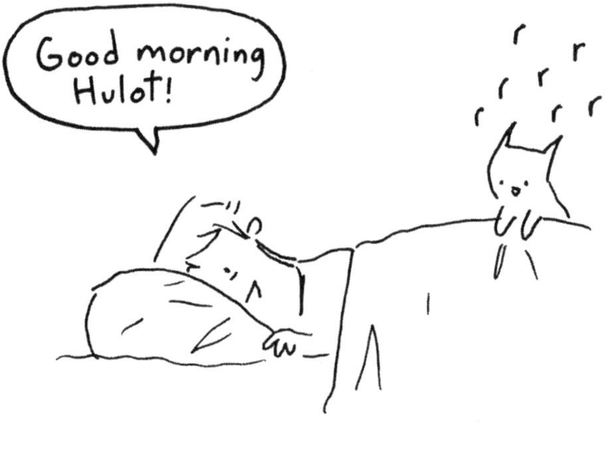
Good morning Hulot!
r r r r r r r r

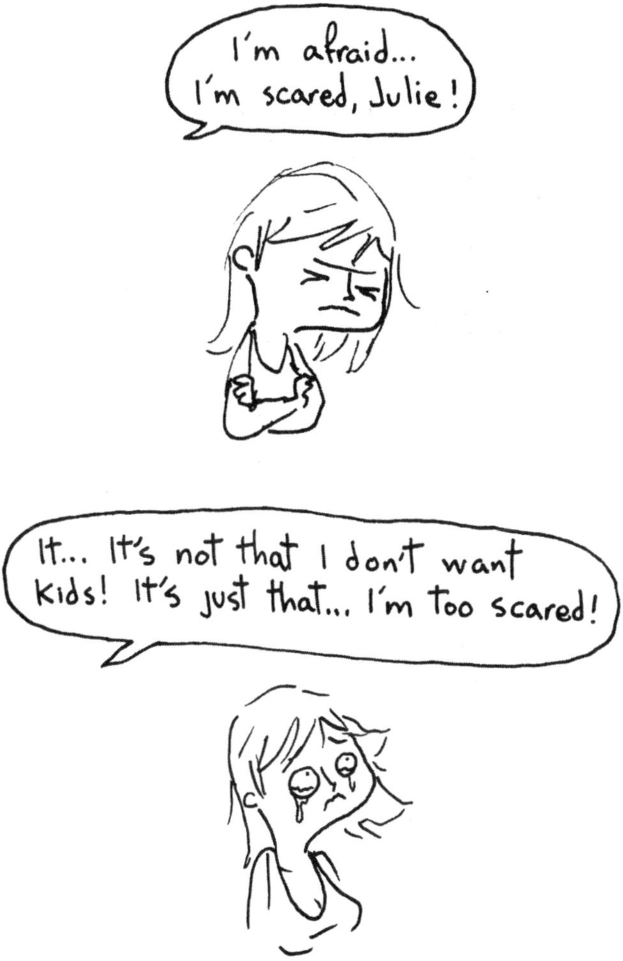
I'm afraid... I'm scared, Julie!
It... It's not that I don't want kids! It's just that... I'm too scared!

I'm afraid he'll be sick!
I'm afraid he'll be unhappy!
I'm afraid he'll be rejected!
I'm afraid he'll reject me!
I'm afraid he'll be depressed!
I'm afraid he'll be like me!
I'm afraid...
I'm afraid he'll die!

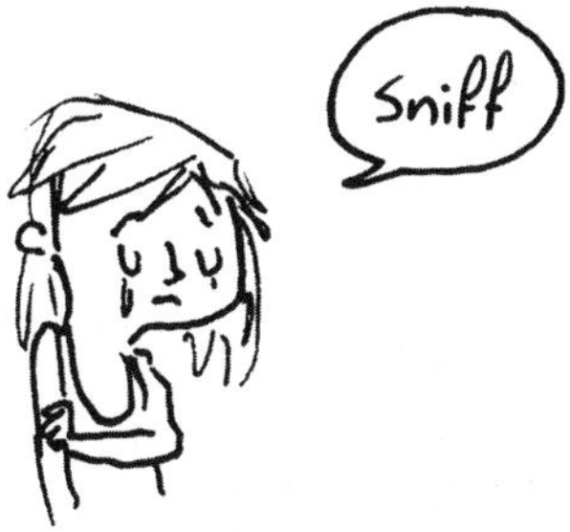
Sniff

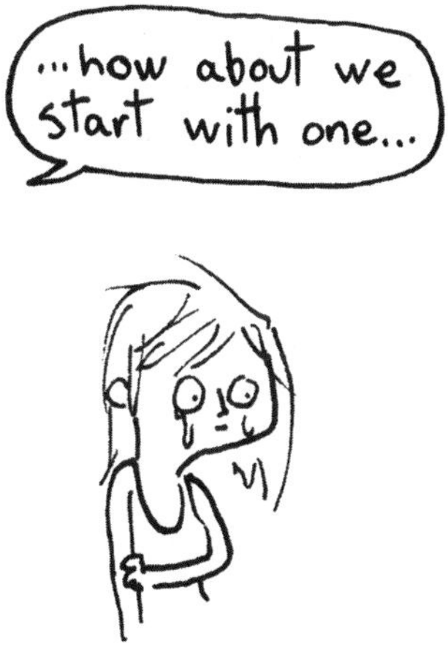
...how about we start with one...

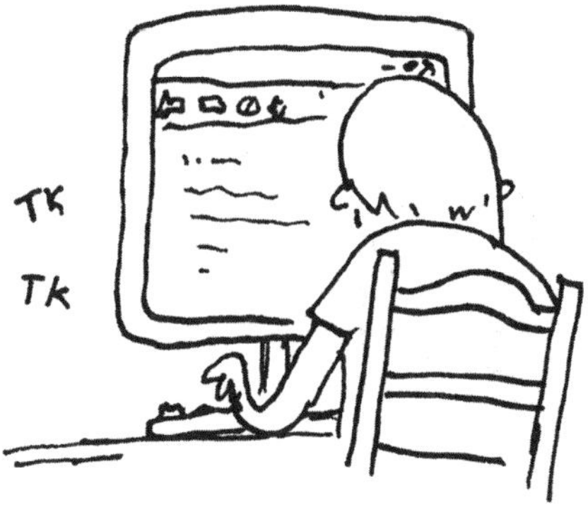
TK
TK

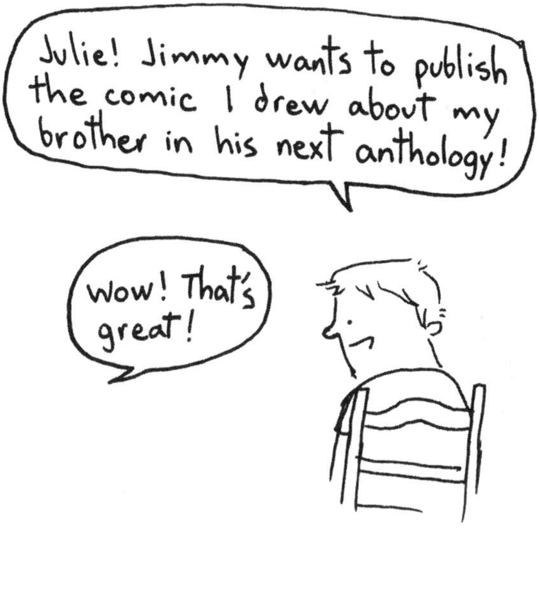
Julie! Jimmy wants to publish the comic I drew about my brother in his next anthology!
Wow! That's great!

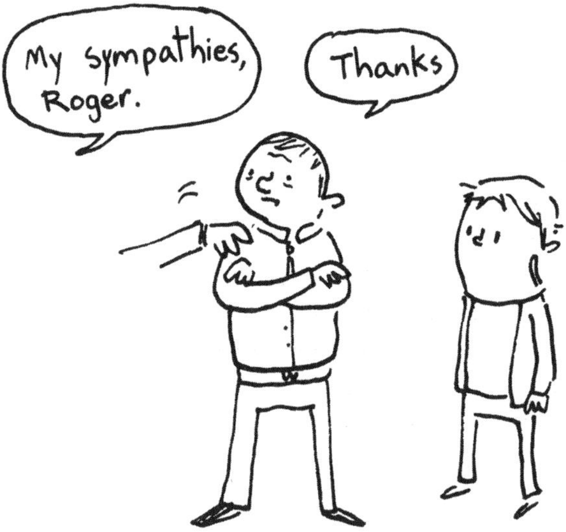
My sympathies, Roger.
Thanks

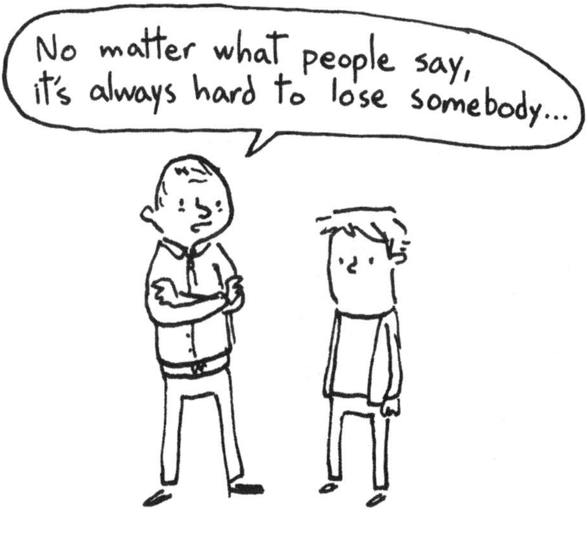
No matter what people say, it's always hard to lose somebody...

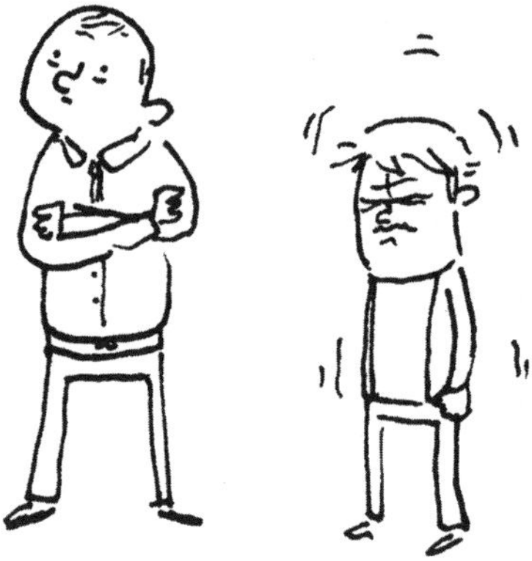

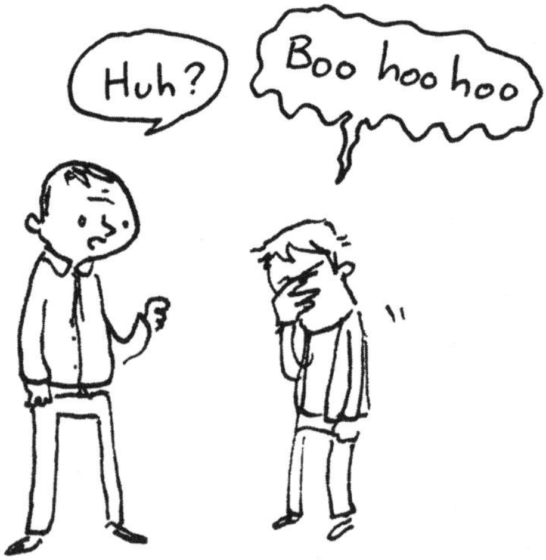
Huh?
Boo hoo hoo

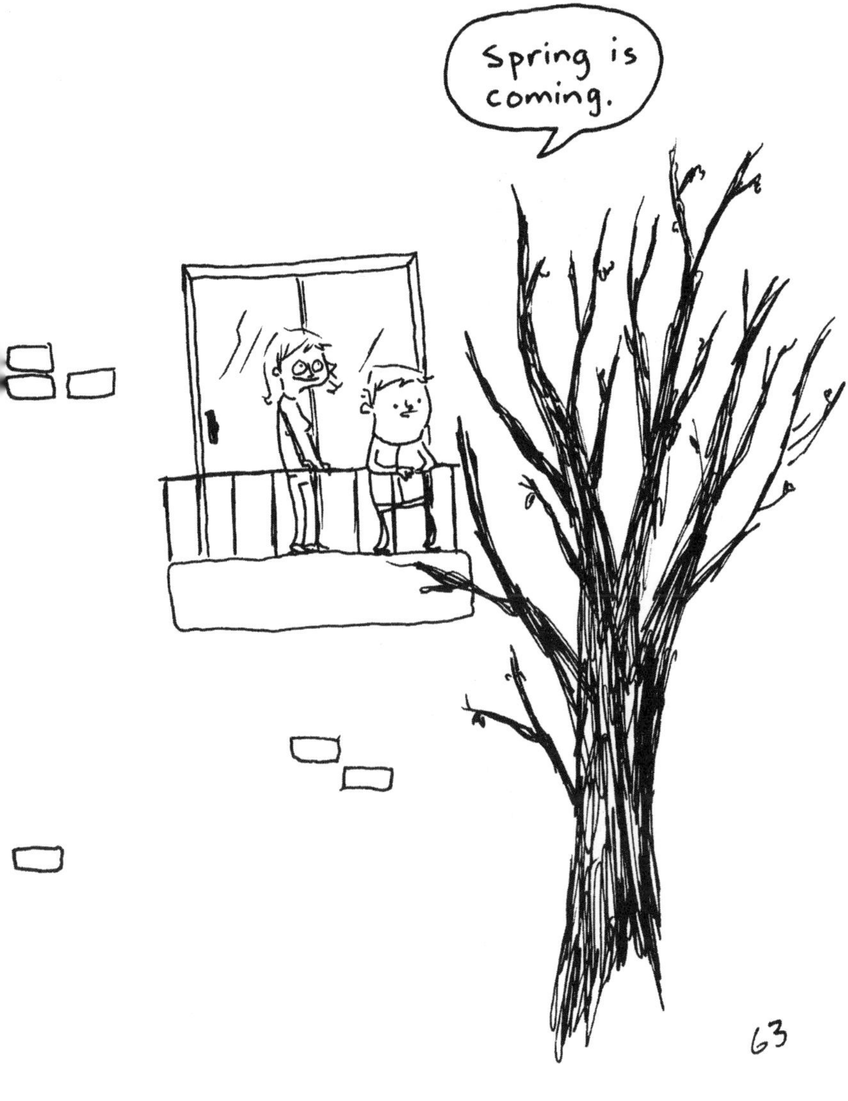
Spring is coming.

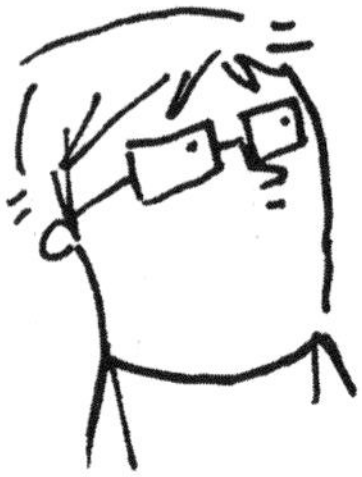

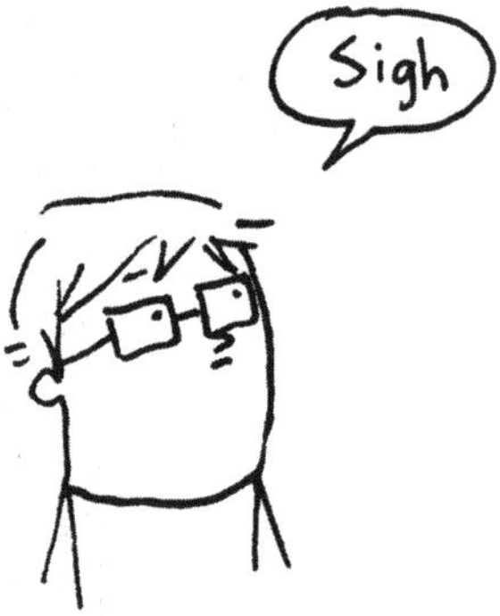
Sigh

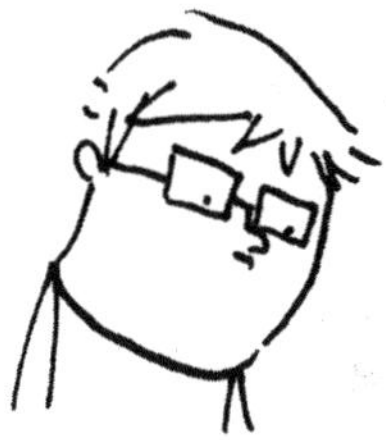

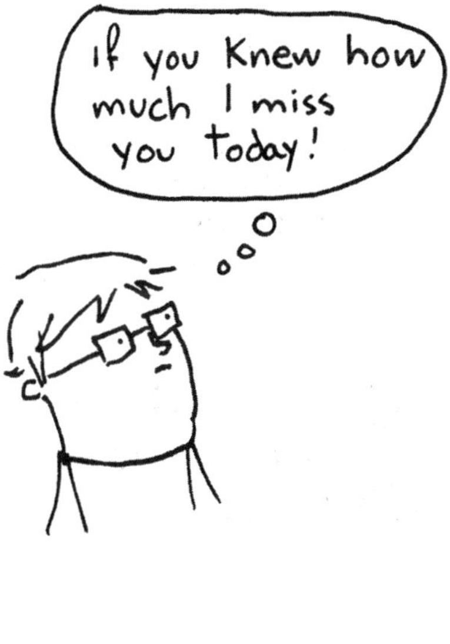
If you knew how much I miss you today!

BEFORE

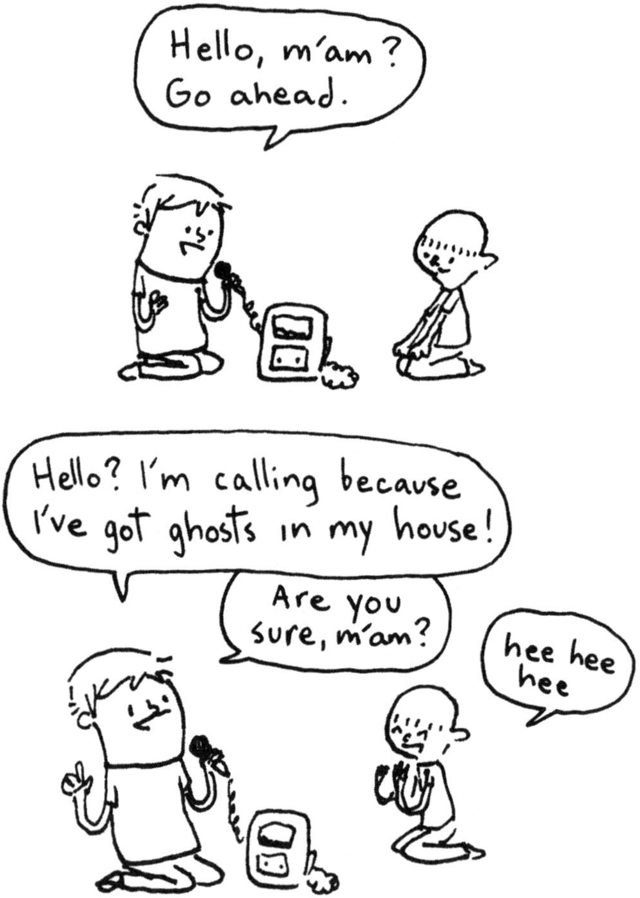
Hello, m'am?
Go ahead.
Hello? I'm calling because
I've got ghosts in my house!
Are you
sure, m'am?
hee hee
hee

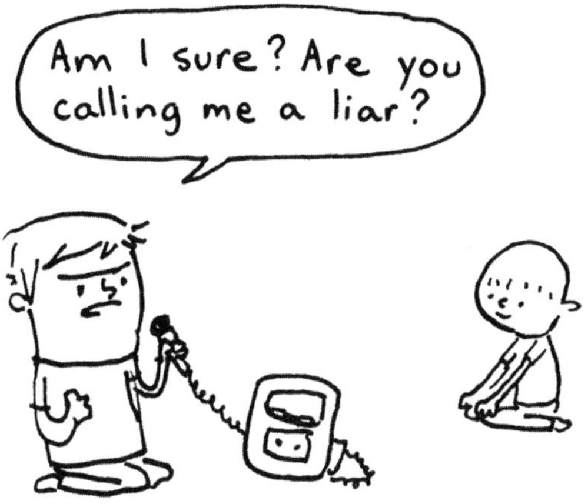
Am I sure? Are you calling me a liar?

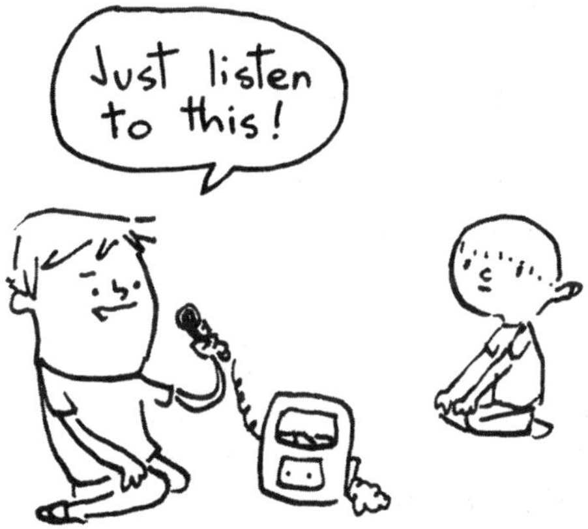
Just listen to this!

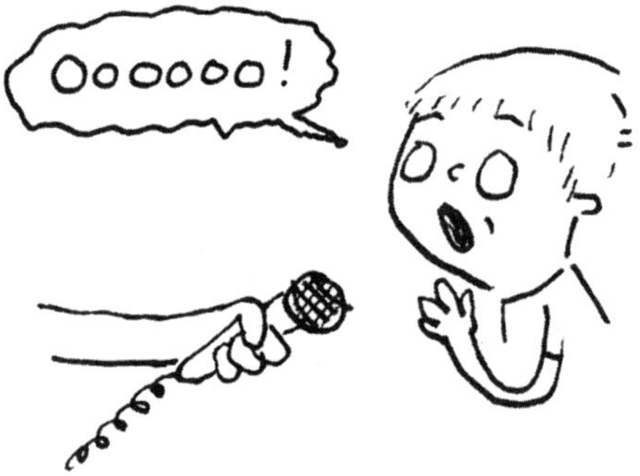
OOOOOO!

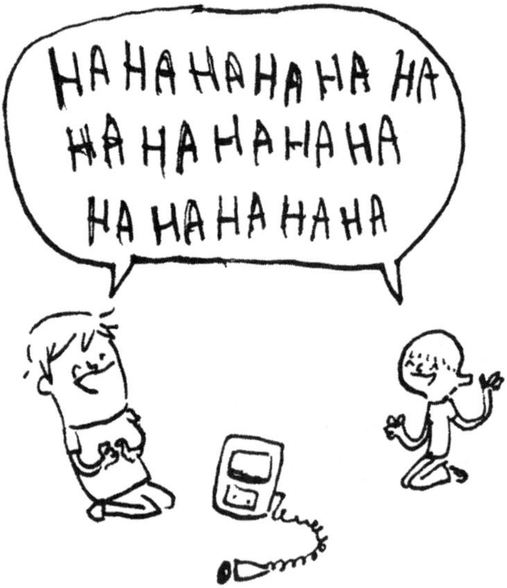
HA HA HA HA HA HA HA
HA HA HA HA HA HA
HA HA HA HA HA HA

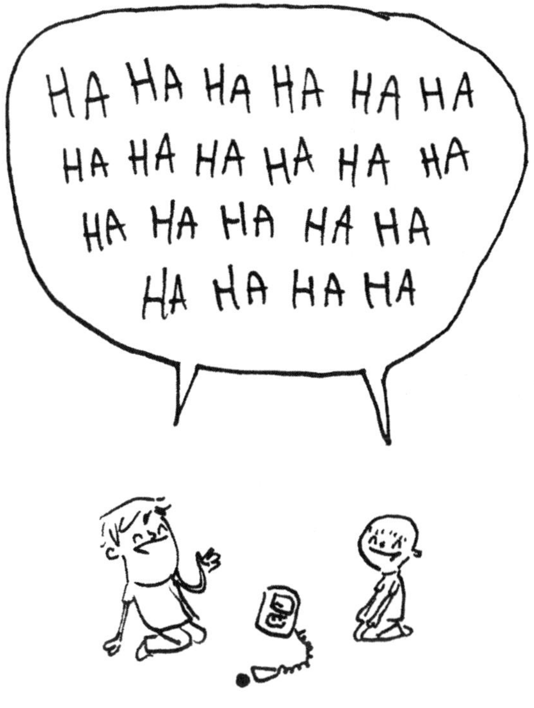
HA HA HA HA HA HA
HA HA HA HA HA HA
HA HA HA HA HA
HA HA HA HA